Writing Theologically

Chap 1 □ pg. 5
5 □ pg. 59
9 □ pg. 119

Writing Theologically

Foundations for Learning

Eric D. Barreto

Fortress Press
Minneapolis

WRITING THEOLOGICALLY

Foundations for Learning

Cover image: Antishock/123RF

Cover design: Laurie Ingram

Library of Congress Cataloging-in-Publication Data

Print ISBN: 978-1-4514-8340-6

eBook ISBN: 978-1-4514-9659-8

The paper used in this publication meets the minimum requirements of American National Standard for Information Sciences — Permanence of Paper for Printed Library Materials, ANSI Z329.48-1984.

Manufactured in the U.S.A.

This book was produced using PressBooks.com, and PDF rendering was done by PrinceXML.

Contents

Contributors

Adam J. Copeland is Director for Theological Inquiry and Administrative-Faculty at Concordia College in Moorhead, Minnesota. An ordained pastor in the Presbyterian Church (USA), he is editor of *Kissing in the Chapel, Praying in the Frat House: Wrestling with Faith and College* (2014) and author of several book chapters on ministry and culture.

David G. Garber Jr. is associate professor of Old Testament and Hebrew at the McAfee School of Theology at Mercer University. He is the author of several articles on the Hebrew prophets and the use of trauma theory as an interpretive stance in biblical studies.

Grace Ji-Sun Kim is visiting researcher at Georgetown University. She is the author of seven books, including *Embracing the Other* (2015), *Contemplations from the Heart* (2014), *Colonialism, Han, and the Transformative Spirit* (2013). She is a co-editor with Dr. Joseph Cheah for the Palgrave Macmillan Book Series "Asian Christianity in Diaspora."

Jacob D. Myers recently completed his PhD at Emory University in homiletics. He has published articles on theology and sexuality, poststructural philosophy, and alternative epistemologies for preaching and worship. He currently teaches adjunctively at Candler School of Theology, Columbia Theological Seminary, and Central Baptist Theological Seminary; he also directs the Summer Institute of Teaching and Learning at Candler School of Theology.

Raj Nadella is assistant professor of New Testament at Columbia Theological Seminary. He is the author of *Dialogue Not Dogma: Many Voices in the Gospel of Luke* (2010) and several articles.

Richard Newton is assistant professor of religious studies at Elizabethtown College. He is a featured blogger at Fortress Academic's Seminarium: The Elements of Great Teaching.

Melinda A. McGarrah Sharp is assistant professor of pastoral theology and ethics at Phillips Theological Seminary in Tulsa, Oklahoma. She is the author of *Misunderstanding Stories: Toward a Postcolonial Pastoral Theology* (2013).

Shively T. J. Smith is assistant professor of New Testament at Wesley Theological Seminary in Washington, DC. She is an elder in the African Methodist Episcopal Church and has contributed to *Feasting on the Gospels* and the Fund for Theological Education Blog.

Karyn L. Wiseman is associate professor of homiletics and director of United Methodist studies at Lutheran Theological Seminary at Philadelphia. She is the author of *I Refuse to Preach a Boring Sermon: Engaging the 21st Century Listener* (2013) and the author of several articles on preaching, liturgy, and digital media in ministry.

Angela Yarber is adjunct professor of women's, gender, and sexuality studies at Wake Forest University. She holds a PhD in Art and Religion from the Graduate Theological Union and is author of *Embodying the Feminine in the Dances of the World's Religions* (2011), *The Gendered Pulpit* (2013), *Dance in Scripture* (2013), *Holy Women Icons* (2014), *Tearing Open the Heavens* (2104), and coauthor of *Microaggressions in Ministry* (forthcoming 2015). For more, visit angelayarber.com.

Introduction

Eric D. Barreto

There is no way around it. Writing is hard, hard work.

As much as we like to romanticize the author and her craft, writing is anything but easy. Even if you are sitting in a beautiful cabin near a placid lake on a beautiful fall day, writing is difficult. Even if you are surrounded by brilliant books in a university library, writing is laborious. Even if you are sitting at a wooden desk and your hand is holding an exquisitely designed fountain pen, writing is a job. Even if you have a powerful tablet and a steaming cup of coffee before you, writing will not just happen without the sweat of your brow and maybe even a few tears along the way.

There are no muses who will inspire you. There is no magic to writing but sitting and writing until the work is done or at least mostly done.

But, trust me, it is not all bad news. That hard, hard work is both necessary and vital to your ministry.

Writing is hard work. And yet so many of us can't help but write. And when we write well, we discover delight. When we can communicate our ideas clearly and persuasively and passionately, we answer the high call to be proclaimers of the good news of Jesus Christ. When we write in a way that shifts someone's perspective from death to life, from hatred to love, from fear to hope, we join a long chorus of witnesses to God's grace for us all.

Writing is labor and joy, difficulty and delight. You could move through your seminary years dreading all the writing you will do. You could see these assignments as obstacles along the path to ministry. You could see weekly sermons and church newsletters as unending burdens. You could see writing as a necessary but burdensome part of your call.

But there is another possibility.

This book hopes to give you a theological vision for your writing. Yes, writing is hard work. Yes, writing can keep us awake at night. Yes, writing can cause more gray hairs to crop up. But writing is also one of the most potent ways we can help cast a vision for a community seeking a way to serve God and neighbor. Writing is one of God's invitations to participate in God's never-ending reign, right here, right now.

The essays in this book are honest about the difficulties of writing, but they also invite you to a spirituality and theology of writing that can nurture and sustain you both in seminary and during a lifetime of ministry. In this book, we confess that, ultimately, writing is not just human activity but a stunning way in which God speaks still today.

To be clear, I'm not saying that everything you and I write are the very words of God. We're not just dictating divine declamations. Instead, writing requires us to be students of God, God's word, God's people, and God's world. A writer listens as much as she writes, reads as much as she composes, lives as much as she declaims.

In this book, a group of thoughtful theologians and scholars condense their wisdom and experiences for you, the potential or new student of theology. You are at the cusp of a life-changing journey of faith and study. You will not emerge the same from these years of formative study. Moreover, the people you will one day serve will change you and form you. Writing is an indispensable way that you can participate and reflect upon these changes in your own life. Writing can help you respond and contribute to communities of learning and faith whether at your theological school or in the communities you will serve.

Some things about writing have changed little over the years. Plato and Shakespeare and Toni Morrison would probably nod in agreement if they had read the preceding paragraphs. But one thing has changed dramatically.

A digital revolution has turned former consumers of media into its producers also. Anyone with a computer and an Internet connection can publish her thoughts and potentially reach a worldwide audience. Publishing has never been easier. Our voices have never echoed so broadly. The Internet is a megaphone for anyone's voice, whether what one is writing is shrill or incisive, deluded or inspired, insipid or insightful.

How then do we write when our world is shrinking and our voices are louder than ever? What words would Jesus have us speak in an ever more divided and divisive world? What can we say that will pierce the din of negativity and hopelessness that so often blare from all the various screens that now populate our everyday lives?

The call is high, the risks great, but so are the resources available to you. This book is a primer for your thinking about writing. With this book, you start a long process of reflection and action.

One of my favorite Twitter accounts is @AdviceToWriters. As the Twitter handle suggests, this account shares insights several times a day about writing. Inspiring quotes from talented writers are oases on days when my writing flow is off. Smart tactics can stir me from my compositional stupor. And yet all these fabulous tweets boil down to a simple reality: writing is perhaps both the hardest and the most satisfying intellectual activity any of us engage in.

Read the essays in the book, reflect on them, and then pick up your pen or your keyboard. You have a voice. God has called you to use it. And you never know what effect your words will have. You never know how God will imbue your feeble words with the power of the Spirit.

And when that happens, you will forget the late nights struggling over that sermon or that time your computer crashed right as you clicked "Save." All you will remember is the power of God to transform a broken world. And then you will become a witness to God's loving and graceful inspiration of ordinary people to imagine an extraordinary world.

Speak. Write. Tell the stories of God's good news. We are waiting and listening. Now it's your turn to write theologically.

1

Writing Basically

Richard Newton

Writing has played a pivotal role in the formation and spread of the Christian witness. In the prologue to the Gospel of John, we find an illuminating image of this relationship. "In the beginning was the Word, and the Word was with God, and the Word was God."[1] The evangelist likens Christ to "the Word" (Greek *ho logos*, think "logic"), the very expression of reason, present since before creation and enlightening the world ever since. The apostle Paul tells the Corinthians that Jesus' passion and resurrection happened "in accordance with the scriptures."[2] These "scriptures" (Greek *tas graphas*, imagine "graphics") or, more literally, "writings" to which Paul refers clearly dictated the dimensions of his worldview. For two millennia the church has used the discipline of writing to work out its understanding of who God is and what God is about. At the most basic level, this is writing theologically. Through this historic

1. John 1:1 NRSV.
2. 1 Cor. 15:3–4 NRSV.

practice, you too—when you write theologically—can join in the body of Christ's ongoing meditation on God's movement in the world.

At the same time, the task of writing has a way of playing on a person's worst fears. Maybe you are haunted by an incident in a previous educational setting. Maybe you are nervous about working in a language in which you are less than comfortable. Perhaps the unfamiliar halls of your seminary echo the quiet voice inside you saying, "You're not a writer."

But writing is not a zero-sum game. You do not fail to write anymore than you fail to live. Writing is a skill to be worked on such that you might enjoy the fruits of your labor. When those called to ministry write well, the world comes to understand better what is good about the good news. As you consider the next step in your vocational journey, ask yourself not whether you can write (for you can), but how willing you are to work at writing more effectively. Isn't the word you are carrying worthy of your best efforts?

In concert with the wider mission of this book, this chapter lays out some basic writing skills that you will have the opportunity to develop throughout seminary. I invite you to use this chapter to consider your own vocational journey and discern how you might prepare to write theologically. Along the way, we will review the types of writing you will do in seminary and some ways you can sharpen your skills. By taking a moment to review the basics of theological writing, we prepare ourselves to express the word residing within us.

What Will I Be Writing?

While we often speak of ministry training in singular terms, a seminary education comprises various courses of study. Biblical interpretation, church history, the role of faith in society, the Christian message in theory and practice: each of these disciplines offers insight into an effective life in ministry. Your professors will use writing as a way to find out what you have learned. For this reason, I recommend that you approach writing assignments not as tests but as opportunities to discover what you can do with new ministerial tools. Writing creates a space to inventory the fruits born out of discipleship and the seeds in need of cultivation. Indeed, writing is hard work. But more important, it is worthwhile work.

The theological writer is challenged with having to inhabit two modes. The first is the *reflexive mode*. This involves finding one's own position on an issue. In the reflexive mode, the seminarian takes inventory of his or her relationship to a subject matter—be it a biblical term or passage (for example, the *logos* in John 1), a theological concept (such as the Trinity), or ministry setting (a congregation, worship community, mission field, or other location). The reflexive mode is a soul-searching activity for the author. This can take place in a personal journal or in a writing circle of fellow journeyers. (See figure 1.)

Figure 1

Examples of Writing Theologically in the Reflexive Mode

Lectio Divina

Historically, "divine reading" refers to the four-part Benedictine practice of reading, meditating, praying, and contemplating a passage of Scripture. More broadly, we might think of this as devotional Bible study carried out in private or in community.

Pastoral Care Diary

This is not only a record of activities done by a minister but also a registry of reactions to ministry events—from counseling sessions to worship services to outreach. The diary chronicles developments in the life of the pastor and the parish.

The Preacher's File

Good sermons (usually) are not written overnight. Preachers are always on the lookout for illustrations, analogies, and interpretations to help their congregations connect with a future message. This file provides a space to jot down quick reflections for you to think through later.

Liturgical Journal

Curating the aesthetic and ritual elements of worship requires a certain level of artistry. Journals provide a space to brainstorm and imagine. The finished product may look dramatically different from one's notes, but the journal eases the troublesome task of getting started.

The second mode is the *critical mode*. This involves shaping another person's perspective on an issue. The seminarian defends a position in a persuasive fashion—that is, a manner that convinces the reader of the argument's validity. In the critical mode, the seminarian is concerned with his or her perspective being understood and endorsed by another person (such as a biblical studies professor, church historian, theologian, fellow classmate, or parishioner). Key here is focusing on the court of readers' opinions. Ultimately, judgment on the effectiveness of the writing lies largely outside the writer's own assessment. (See figure 2.)

Figure 2

Examples of Writing Theologically in the Critical Mode

Credo

From the Latin for "I believe," a credo paper puts forth a coherent statement of the Christian faith, justifying the author's belief with support from a range of sources that include history, current events, Scripture, and the witness of other Christians.

Biblical Exegesis

Exegesis refers to scriptural interpretation based upon what is known from the text and its historical context. With the help of specialized dictionaries, encyclopedias, and scholarly commentaries, these papers advance theological ways of reading a biblical passage.

Church History Paper

These writings explore specific moments in the life of the church, characterizing noteworthy events in which Christians have struggled to work out their faith. Rather than taking a side in a debate, you might be more likely to discuss how each side understood their actions as faithful.

Social Analysis Essay

In these papers, you might thoroughly discuss a problem typical to your ministry setting and prescribe a course of action. Your approach to these controversies will reflect your study of the human condition, your theological convictions, and your practice of the ministerial arts.

Liturgical Write-Up

The word *liturgy* derives from a Greek term meaning "work of the people" and usually refers to the rituals, services, and artistic aspects of Christian worship. While liturgy is commonly associated with the reflexive mode, liturgical design involves a critical weighing of church tradition, cultural literacy, and ministerial wisdom.

Part of what makes theological education unique is the high esteem in which both the reflexive and the critical modes are held. Seminaries unequivocally want their students to succeed. After all, the Latin term *seminarium* refers to a "seedbed," a place for nurturing. That being said, you, your fellow students, and your teachers are obligated to prune understandings that hinder the church from growing in spirit and truth. Even when done in the most constructive way, criticism can be difficult to take. As you receive feedback, think through how you can respond gracefully and fruitfully to criticism and praise alike.

In the end, the biggest obstacle to the theological writer may be the self. Many seminarians see themselves as either good writers or bad writers. Both of these attitudes can be dangerous. The former leads you to believe that your work glows even when it doesn't. The self-proclaimed latter can't see the potential in their own work. I encourage you to remember that all writers have good days and bad days, but good writing begins with a commitment to the demands of the craft.

How Can I Write Well?

When writing in the reflexive mode, you are usually the judge and jury on the quality of your expression. But when writing in the critical mode, your readers will evaluate your work. So, what does good critical writing look like? In some respects, the answer is going to vary depending on your reader's taste.

Readers are fickle. Some of us appreciate long, complex sentences. Others like terse prose. Style and grammar conventions will also depend on the context of a writer's audience. Professors will usually outline their expectations by referring you to specific handbooks, manuals, or rubrics. In the case that he or she does not list this in a syllabus, ask your professors, your fellow students, or your campus writing center for some recommended resources.

Knowing your readers' preferences on these matters is important, but truth be told, they are secondary to one defining question: *Did you convince the reader that you know what you're talking about?* Writing well is contingent upon making your reader answer affirmatively. This result is different from convincing your reader that you are correct. Although that may be ideal, your reader may reserve the right to maintain another equally sound perspective. Good writing can leave room for other valid opinions. And this is also different from captivating your reader with your beautiful prose. While you must keep your audience's attention, there is such a thing as artful nonsense. Smooth writing cannot make up for a lack of substance. You want readers to finish your work thinking, "Now that was thought provoking!"

At some point in your educational career, you were likely exposed to any number of writing models. Though they differ in terminology and emphasis, most of these approaches overlap in their intent to help you present a coherent argument. As a teacher, I want my students to tell me in the most efficient way possible what they think and why they think it. It is important to structure your writing in such a way that your reader can follow along easily. As you start your seminary education, it might be helpful to review what the three major parts of a paper—the introduction, body, and conclusion—are trying to accomplish.

The Get-to-the-Point Introduction

Introductions are the workhorse of any piece of writing. Writers are expected to lay out the subject of interest, the core argument, and argument structure in such a way that the reader will want to continue reading. To further complicate matters, these expectations are to be met in a relatively short section of the work. This call for clarity prompts many authors to rush through this principal portion of the writing process, but if done dutifully, the introduction can lay the foundation for your most impressive work. (See figure 3.)

While all this sounds like a tall order, it becomes quite manageable (and even helpful) when you see the forest for the trees. The point of an introduction is to tell readers what you have learned about a subject after giving it some serious thought. They need to know these three things:

- Your *topic* or the subject matter of your paper. This is the search string your reader would use to find your paper and other related works at the library or on the Internet.
- Your *research question* or the issue you are raising about your topic. This is the specific who, what, where, why, when, how you are asking about your chosen topic.
- Your *thesis statement* or the answer to your research question. This is the informed response that you are prepared to give as a result of your study of the topic and issue.

In addition to presenting information central to your paper, you'll find that writing a successful introduction clarifies your thought process, enticing you to think about how all the different elements of your argument work together.

For example, if I were to write a critical paper on writing critically in seminary, I would need to raise an *issue* about my topic that would be worthy of investigation. After all, who would want to read (let alone, write!) something of little interest? So, for a research question, I might ask, "Why is it important for seminarians to learn how to write well?" Now having raised this question, the reader is going to expect me to answer it. This is where the thesis statement comes into play: "By surfacing the importance of rationality in the Fourth Gospel and the role of Scripture in the theology of the apostle Paul, seminarians should understand critical writing as a central and commendable part of the Christian witness."

Figure 3

Breaking Down the Get to the Point Introduction

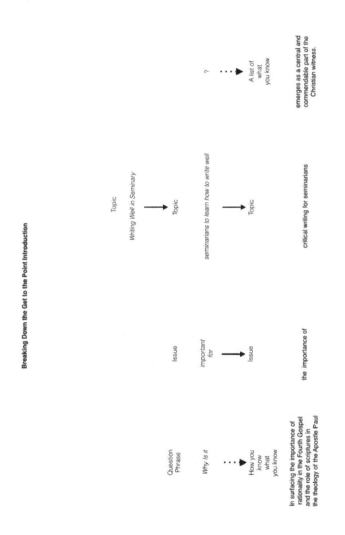

As shown above, the introduction gives a blueprint of your main argument. Notice how you can see the topic and issue consistently throughout each respective step. This moves the reader from your fascinating question to your insightful answer, which is the point of a strong introduction.

✓ACE Body Paragraphs

This exploration of good critical writing began with the goal of learning how to convince readers that you know what you're talking about. You now know a good introduction is where you lay out what you want to discuss, but how do you go about convincing a reader of the validity of your case? Readers will expect you to expand on the points that I just listed in describing the introduction. And in addition to needing to know from where you are getting your information, readers will want to be able to follow your train of thought. These demands are tailor-made for the paragraphs in the body section of a paper. If constructed well, you are on the way to a coherent argument. You just have to remember the three functions of what I call ACE body paragraphs. (See figure 4.)

Body paragraphs *assert* your views on your chosen topic and issue. A thesis statement is in fact an assertion, because you are saying that you claim to know some things about the topic and issue. Whenever you define something, show a correlation, suggest a cause, or put forward an interpretation, you have asserted your perspective. In each body paragraph, you will begin by showcasing a piece of your thesis statement for your readers' consideration. When brainstorming your first body paragraph, ask yourself what is the first idea you need to establish for your reader. Given our previous example, one might set out by asserting the importance of rationality in the Fourth Gospel. The rest of one's thesis can be developed in subsequent body paragraphs, but this assertion will act as the starting point and sole focus of my paragraph.

Naturally, readers are going to wonder why you are confident in your assertion. This is why body paragraphs provide *evidence*. Evidence comprises all the experts, books, articles, and examples you use to support your assertion. Without evidence, your reader will presume that your paragraph's assertion is a made-up opinion rather than a demonstrable argument. For instance, imagine a reader questioning the importance of rationality in the Fourth Gospel. For the claim to hold water, one would need to back up that assertion. This could be done with a reference to the prologue to the Gospel of John. One might quote Luke Timothy Johnson, a New Testament scholar, who describes its author as crafting a "symbolic world" that combines abstract images like "'light,' 'truth,' and 'life'" with actions such as "'believing,' 'seeing,' and 'knowing.'"[3] From these two pieces of evidence, the reader will begin to see the rationale behind the assertion, even if his or her understanding of the argument is still developing.

That being said, good writing doesn't leave the reader's comprehension to chance. I suspect you know what it is like to read fact after fact and wonder, "So what's all of this supposed to mean?" Commentary keeps the reader caught up, making plain how the evidence contributes to the assertion's validity. It is the explanation, elaboration, interpretation, and analysis you use to illustrate your point. Your commentary (C) reinforces the link between your assertion (A) and evidence (E) for your readers: $A \leftarrow C \rightarrow E$. Put differently, your commentary ensures that your reader does not get lost in the depth of your point (assertion) and the breadth of your data (evidence). So, if I want to highlight the relevance of the prologue to

---

3. Luke Timothy Johnson, *The Writings of the New Testament: An Interpretation*, rev. ed. (Minneapolis: Fortress Press, 1999), 526.

the Gospel of John to the importance of Christian writing, it would be helpful for the reader to learn that the Greek term *logos*—which English translations frequently render as "the Word"—is retained in English in more familiar terms like *logic* and *logo*, both of which signify approaches to human understanding. Likewise, readers would benefit from a paraphrase of Professor Johnson's statement, which suggested that the evangelist's intention to describe more theoretical matters parallels his understanding of the Word that became flesh. Hence, the reader is going to have a much greater chance of seeing written expression as a major touchstone for the Gospel author.

Figure 4

Breaking Down the ACE Body Paragraph

Assertion: Think "I argue . . ." statements.[4]

- Types: causes, correlations, opinions, your observations, and your suggestions
- Function: Describe how this helps demonstrate your thesis statement.
- This is the only idea that you are trying to teach your reader in this paragraph.
- If you have included more than one idea, you need to have more than one ACE. If there's nothing to argue, then it is likely not an assertion but commentary or evidence.[5]

4. Professors are divided over the appropriateness of the first-person pronoun in academic writing. Regardless, "I argue" makes a helpful prompt for your assertions. You can use the first-person pronoun to get you started and then erase it after you establish your assertion. Your sentence will nearly always work without the first-person clause.
5. If your paragraph primarily presents the argument of another writer, your assertion can be

Evidence: Think, "He, she, it, they argue[s] . . . " statements.

- Types: studies, definitions, images, quotations, others' observations and suggestions

- Function: Briefly note how you intend for this to help you defend your assertion.

- Remember, when summarizing, paraphrasing, or quoting a passage, a source must be cited.

- This is corroborated information, not your own ideas.[6]

Commentary: Think, "Thus, you, the reader, should now understand . . . "

- Types: analysis, interpretation ("This means . . . "), elaboration, explanation

- Function: How does this connect your evidence to the assertion?

- No evidence should be placed here.

- This is where you showcase your understanding of the evidence and how it proves your assertion.

More than a writing rubric, ACE body paragraphs aid you in keeping the reader in mind.

It is a mentality that foregrounds what you claim to know (your assertions), how you know it (your evidence), and how your reader

thought of as your interpretation of that writer's work. Thus, "Gonzales surmises . . . " can serve as an assertion if you are planning on walking the reader through the argument.

6. I tell my students that only those who have performed a peer-reviewed study may cite themselves as evidence. If you feel the need to cite yourself, discuss the matter with your teacher. You may be instructed to find an established resource that makes your desired point.

can better grasp it (your commentary). Theological writing is about sharing with your reader what you have come to understand about God's activity. Thus, body paragraphs are the building blocks of greater insights and greater exchange.

The Get-Out-of-the-Way Conclusion

Once you have explained your reasoning, your reader will judge for him- or herself the validity of your argument. This sounds like a cold proposition, but I think it best to treat this like a parting of companions. With conclusions, you may be tempted to linger—sneaking in one or two more points, adding a neat detail here, or throwing in a reference there. But you're better off getting out of the way and leaving the reader with the time and space to appreciate your work.

That is not to say your conclusion can't leave a lasting impression. You can begin by restating your thesis statement, which will make more sense now that your reader is familiar with your argument. In the case of the earlier example, this could look something like, "By reading the Gospel of John and the Pauline witness, we are reminded that writing is a foundational part of our Christian heritage." You might then remind the reader why you made the argument in the first place, reiterating the question that spurred your research. Since our research question asked whether it was important for seminarians to learn how to write, the conclusion brings the reader to consider this issue in light of the provided information. And finally, your reader should be left with a sense of why these ideas matter—in our case, the notion that writing is historically tied to the Christian witness. Your paper will have come full circle, and your reader will, you hope, appreciate your hard work.

How Can I Write Better?

Theological writing, particularly in the critical mode, is a lot of work. Even as I was laying out what it entails, I was thinking to myself, "Am I really up for this?" But remember what this is. We are talking about the mantle of leadership represented by whatever degree or certification you are working toward. At journey's end, you will be a trusted theological authority in your community. We ought to learn to write well because we believe in the significance of the message we carry for ourselves and to others.

In my years as a former seminarian, minister, and professor, I have observed some best practices among theological writers of all levels. They read widely and often, keeping abreast of happenings in the world and church. They share their writing with colleagues, actively seeking critical feedback. And they see writing as part of their calling. Crafting expressions of the Christian message is central to their livelihood.

We write theology the way doctors practice medicine. Before us is serious work that we will never fully master. But we can gracefully and dutifully practice writing in hopes that we will help perfect the body of Christ.

2

Writing Persuasively

David G. Garber Jr.

Everywhere we turn, we hear the voices of people arguing. If we flip on the news, we see talking heads barking sound bites at one another. When we scroll through our social media feeds, we find friends or family from one camp or the other regurgitating certain political, social, or religious one-liners. Arguing is cultural. Arguing is entertainment. Arguing can even be fun for certain types of people. But making an argument is also countercultural. Taking into consideration opposing viewpoints and thinking through all the implications of your perspective is an arduous process. If we are going to be mindful about our service to God, the church, and the world, however, we must learn how to communicate persuasively while elevating the culture of dialogue with our neighbor, leading to a posture of reconciliation with all of God's children.

The Biblical Roots of Rhetoric

Arguments, indeed, have biblical roots. In Genesis 18, Abraham engages YHWH in a persuasive argument. After God reveals intentions to destroy the city of Sodom, Abraham challenges God's notion of justice, asking, in essence, the question of collateral damage: "Will you indeed sweep away the righteous with the wicked?" (Gen. 18:23).[1] His language is even more forceful in verse 25:

> Far be it from you to do such a thing, to slay the righteous with the wicked, so that the righteous fare as the wicked! Far be that from you! Shall not the Judge of all the earth do what is just?

Notice that Abraham knows his audience well. He is speaking to YHWH, the creator and ruler of all, who initially called him to migrate to Canaan. Knowing his audience, he precedes each of his challenges with an acknowledgment of his status before the creator. At times he offers, "Let me take it upon myself to speak to the Lord, I who am but dust and ashes" (v. 27, cf. Job 30:19 and 42:6). Recognizing how annoying his persistence may appear, he begs, "Oh do not let the Lord be angry if I speak just once more" (v. 30). After a lengthy series of questions that whittles down the number of possible righteous in the city from fifty, to forty-five, to forty, thirty, twenty, and finally ten, God acquiesces to all of Abraham's requests. Abraham consistently appeals to God's concern for the righteous in each of his questions, fulfilling the promise that Abraham would be a blessing to the nations by pleading on their behalf to the very God who seeks to destroy them.

Similarly, in Exodus 32, Moses argues with God in favor of the wayward Israelites who had just constructed and worshiped the golden calf. In this text, God threatens to consume the Israelites in

---

1. All Scripture citations are from the New Revised Standard Version.

the fires of divine wrath (v. 10). Moses, however, intercedes. Moses' argument consists of two tactics: an appeal to God's reputation and an appeal to God's integrity. Moses appeals to God's reputation by asking what the Egyptians might say if they hear of God's destruction of the Israelites in the wilderness. Would they wonder why God took such great pains to liberate the Israelites only to obliterate them? Would they consider God evil? Second, Moses appeals to God's integrity regarding the promise God made to the ancestors of Israel. Would God revoke God's word by annihilating the people of the promise in the wilderness? Moses' arguments are successful and preserve both God's reputation in the eyes of the nations and the people of Israel (Exod. 32:11–14). Abraham and Moses teach us that the art of persuasion does not simply involve changing minds but can also serve as an act of intercessory prayer, reconciling us with our neighbors.

Abraham's and Moses' willingness to speak persuasively to God foreshadows the work of the prophets who follow in their tradition. The prophets were masters of rhetoric. Sometimes their rhetoric was successful and sometimes it was not, yet the prophets remained true to their prophetic task of persuasion. Amos, standing in the tradition of Moses, twice intercedes on behalf of the people when God seeks to destroy them, asking of the wroth deity, "O Lord GOD, forgive, I beg you! How can Jacob stand? He is so small!" (Amos 7:2, 5). In both instances, YHWH relents and holds back the punishment.[2] In contrast, Isaiah unsuccessfully attempts to persuade Ahaz to trust God during the siege against Jerusalem led by Pekah and Rezin. Even though Isaiah's argument involves a sign from God and an appeal to faithfulness, ultimately Ahaz refuses to listen,

---

2. This is not the case with the two visions that follow in Amos 7:7–9 and 8:1–3. The intervening narrative in Amos 7:10–17 depicts the priest Amaziah hell-bent on silencing the prophet. In so doing, perhaps he silences the only voice who might intercede on Israel's behalf.

leading Judah to become a vassal state of the Assyrian empire (Isa. 7:7-17). Jeremiah likewise contends with the kings Jehoiakim and Zedekiah, both of whom ignore the pleas of the prophet to do justice and to submit to the authority of Babylon (for example, Jeremiah 28 and 34). It can be tempting to set aside the prophetic call to speak persuasively for certain causes or about certain issues that face the church and society. These prophets, however, serve as a model for current and future ministers of the gospel to heed the call to communicate persuasively, regardless of the possible outcome. Our contemporary world, filled with cruelty and contention, draws us to remain faithful and to emulate such prophetic rhetoric even in the face of seemingly insurmountable objection.

In some instances, seminarians altruistically shy away from making an argument in fear that it would somehow be manipulative. Indeed, some examples from the biblical narrative highlight the craftiness of certain figures in persuading their audiences. This is the case with the first debate in the Bible. The serpent in the garden is the craftiest of all creatures and uses the art of questioning to persuade the first humans to eat of the tree of knowledge: "Did God say, 'You shall not eat from any tree in the garden'?" (Gen. 3:1).

Craftiness does not necessitate deception, but it does sometimes involve the spinning of a good tale. In confronting David about his sins of murder and adultery, Nathan relays a parable about a rich man who steals a poor man's only lamb to serve a traveler, even though the rich man had plenty of resources in his own flock. David immediately condemns the man, at which point the prophet reveals the allegory as an example of what David himself had done by taking Bathsheba as his own wife and killing Uriah. Likewise, the wise woman of Tekoa in 2 Samuel 14 puts on a ruse, following Joab's instructions. After Absalom kills his brother, she comes to David dressed in mourning clothes and posing as a widow, conveying a story concerning one of her two sons who killed the other. The bloodthirsty family seeks the life of the murderer, an action that would leave the widow bereft of an heir. David decrees forgiveness, at which point the woman urges him to take his own advice and be merciful to Absalom. Her successful persuasion leads to a short-lived respite in the turmoil between father and son. From the wise woman of Tekoa and Nathan—and perhaps even the serpent—we learn the importance of perfecting the craft of persuasion to improve our effectiveness.

Rhetoric is not the purview only of prophetic characters or the books that bear their names. The entire book of Job consists of poetic arguments that are as raucous and perhaps even as entertaining as the cacophony we might witness on the cable news cycle. Job argues with his friends and, ultimately, with God. Despite the lack of a *winner* in this book about radical suffering, God still declares Job as one who has spoken the truth about God, unlike Eliphaz the Temanite (Job 42:8). Jesus, too, follows these prophetic and sapiential traditions in the Gospels in his encounters with religious leaders and even in his conversations with God. One of his final pleas in the Gospel of Luke echoes the cries of Moses and Amos, as he intercedes on behalf of his own crucifiers, "Father, forgive them for they know not what they do" (Luke 23:34). Each of these biblical characters engages in rhetoric, the art of persuasion, just as much as our contemporaries do. The need for persuasion is somehow integral to our human existence, an existence seemingly characterized by the desperate need to negotiate conflict. Each of these biblical examples also suggests that attending to the necessity and craft of persuasive communication is an expression of our faithfulness as Christians as well as our commitment toward honest dialogue with our sisters and brothers within the Christian community and beyond.

Barriers to Reconciliatory Rhetoric

Persuasive communication assumes points and counterpoints. It almost invites the participants in the dialogue to be oppositional. But is there room in the reconciliatory mission of the church to be oppositional, even with words? I have often found myself coaching students to deal with their "opponents" when writing on a particular topic. Some students occasionally challenge the idea that Christians should "argue" or even speak in oppositional terms. They suggest that the language of opposition is inherently too confrontational. Even the thought of oppositional language introduces the idea of conflict that many might simply want to avoid for the sake of peace and unity. This conundrum often leads to weak rhetoric accompanied by a chorus of apologetic qualifiers such as, "it seems to me," "in my opinion," or "I think." While the impulse here might be one of altruistic humility, such qualifiers weaken the confidence of your prose, sacrificing the potential impact your voice might have on a variety of topics. Is there a way, however, to embrace a reconciliatory posture in our rhetoric without sacrificing the force our rhetoric needs if it is to effect any change?

Perhaps this is where Christian rhetoric can become truly countercultural.

If we are to embrace a reconciliatory posture in our rhetoric, we need to write in a way that takes into account differing viewpoints fairly while not sacrificing our own well-informed convictions. One of the most pervasive logical fallacies in our culture—and in my experience of having read hundreds of pages of theological student writing—falls under the category of ad hominem. *Ad hominem* is a Latin phrase, literally meaning "against the human."[3] It is a

---

3. When dissecting language and arguments, you must also be aware of how certain approaches might work in certain contexts but may derail your point in other contexts. I recently read a thread on Facebook in which a former student correctly called his opponent's argument an

diversionary tactic often employed to win an argument. Rather than dissecting the logic of the argument or treating the issues involved, an ad hominem approach smears the character of the person who is making the argument. One may, for example, suggest that William has no authority to speak on the topic of penalties for drug possession because William is himself a recovering addict. Here, rather than focusing on William's logic, the opponent discredits his character. Returning momentarily to biblical examples of argumentation, the first debate might illumine the nature and definition of the ad hominem argument. When Eve claims that she and her husband are not allowed even to touch the fruit, the serpent retorts, "You will not die; for God knows that when you eat of it your eyes will be opened, and you will be like God, knowing good and evil." Notice how the serpent in this argument attacks the integrity of his opponent, God.[4]

Ad hominem approaches take many forms in theological student writing, the most egregious of which often reflect denominational or interreligious stereotypes. Students sometimes marvel when they hear various scholars—who make interpretive claims so very different from the student's own personal embedded theology—call themselves Christian. In other cases, entering theology students have dismissed an argument simply because the author is of a different denominational or religious affiliation. A reconciliatory posture to our rhetoric, however, would require us to avoid such personal attacks while also encouraging us to represent the approach of our opposition fairly. While our cultural context likes to employ labels such as conservative, fundamentalist, traditional, liberal, progressive,

---

ad hominem approach. While his evaluation was correct, the use of the Latin term in a casual thread hindered this student's credibility in the eyes of his dialogue partner. Essentially, his dialogue partner considered him pretentious and condescending, creating a further barrier to helpful and persuasive communication.

4. Notice also that the serpent relies on an element of truth that gives credibility to his argument. God does want to preserve the barrier between human and divine. Also, while the first couple eventually dies, their deaths are not immediate.

feminist, Republican, or Democrat in order to reduce the person making an argument to a generalized and manageable caricature, this impulse does not take into account the full humanity of the person behind the argument. Rather than reducing our opposition to an essence, a reconciliatory posture toward rhetoric would suggest eschewing caricatures for close, fair consideration of our opponents' perspectives, focusing on the content of their argument rather than aspects of their personality.

A second logical fallacy that often detracts from persuasive theological writing with a reconciliatory posture is the slippery slope argument. This fallacy, at its best, fosters a faith that attempts to protect the most treasured of its values with ideological barriers or lines in the sand beyond which one dare not tread. The most significant slippery slope arguments in recent times and in certain contexts have been about gender and sexuality issues. Recent arguments about same-sex marriage, for example, often ask, "What's next?" Proponents of these arguments proceed to talk about sexual deviancies such as bestiality or polygamy in a manner that equates these practices with the practices of same-sex couples. The assumption here is that acceptance of same-sex partnerships might lead to the acceptance of any other sexual arrangement that might deviate from the cultural norm. Proponents of this idea worry that Christian culture might deem everything permissible if it concedes on the issue of same-sex partnerships. Raising the potential of these extreme forms of sexual abnormality becomes a diversionary tactic, a red herring, that prevents those engaging in the discussion about gender and sexuality from focusing on interpreting the biblical passages, tradition, and church teaching alongside conversations taking place in the realms of gender studies, psychology, and physiology. Such a distraction has the potential for stalling a conversation that has immediate consequences for many people in our society who self-identify outside the boundaries of heteronormativity. In essence, we may potentially reach detrimental conclusions on the matters of gender and sexuality motivated by the fear of imagined questions beyond the scope of a single issue.

A final logical fallacy common to theology students and that potentially blocks the progress toward reconciliatory persuasion is the appeal to authority. This becomes particularly problematic in religious perspectives that adhere to many authorities, depending on the denomination. Indeed, individual churches and interpreters have to negotiate several authorities in drawing doctrinal and ethical conclusions, including, but not limited to, the Bible, tradition, denominational teaching, doctrine, confessional statements, communal infrastructures, and the Holy Spirit.[5] My experience of student writing additionally suggests that a student's educational culture has ingrained a type of research in which students draw their conclusions and then mine the literature for authorities in the field who might say something relatively supportive. Research, however, is not about simply gathering the statistics or scholars who support a conclusion and arranging them sycophantically as the yes men or yes women for the argument. Thorough research is about dialogue with the scholars, not using them as backup singers for our own agenda.

Conversely, some theology students abdicate their voice entirely to the scholars insomuch as they simply quote, paraphrase, or summarize scholarship in their essays without developing a voice of their own. At worst, this type of writing appears to the reader as laziness, using quotes and paraphrases as filler for the essay in order to reach a minimum page count. At best, a writer who relies too heavily on

5. One might, for example, argue that my recitation of biblical narratives above constitutes an appeal to the Bible as an authority, which would be quite natural given my Baptist denominational background. I intend, however, for my biblical interpretation here to be merely illustrative by using some familiar and unfamiliar narratives from a shared tradition, and I am not suggesting that persuasion in its essence is biblical.

quotation and paraphrase could mistake this approach for humility when it is actually a lack of confidence. The God who has called us as mediators in Christian community has not called us simply to be parrots of earlier authorities but to exercise our own unique capacities for rational thought and creativity as God's agents in this world. Blind appeals to authority mirror the ad hominem fallacy insofar as this type of logic depends on the character or credentials of those cited rather than on the force of the rhetoric on its own merit. In short, a reconciliatory persuasive model leaves no room for either vilification (ad hominem) or idolatry (appeal to authority).[6]

Responding Creatively to the Christian Duty to Persuasive Communication

Writing persuasively, even (or especially) in seminary, does not preclude writing creatively. This is where clear attention to the audience is necessary. When writing an academic paper for a seminary professor, the writer will probably not want to rely on stories but on supporting evidence (facts), research (dialogue with other scholars), and primary texts (the Bible, creeds, confessions, writings of early Christians, and so forth). It may not be the appropriate time to break out your own knack for spinning a tale or your propensity for flowery language. However, when writing persuasively for the church, say in a sermon, you may indeed want to show an ability to relay a moral truth in a short narrative. In writing a persuasive letter to a congregation or denominational body, depending on the context, it may be appropriate to report a short testimonial. In short, writing persuasively involves knowing the audience and what may or may not engage them in the dialogue. This type of persuasion necessitates creative discernment as to how

6. These three examples of logical fallacies are obviously not exhaustive but illustrative.

best to convey a perspective. While theology students often feel the need to bracket their creativity in biblical, theological, or historical studies, certain assignments even in these disciplines might provide avenues to explore and hone such creative skills.[7]

Finally, writing with an eye toward reconciliatory persuasion will demand that theology students, ministers, and scholars continue to think creatively and counterculturally in order to communicate within a politically, theologically, and ideologically polarized climate. Too often, Christians in the broader culture have allowed themselves to be trapped by caricatures and marginalized as irrelevant voices. With the problems of war, famine, disease, and other ailments facing the human community, rational and persuasive Christian voices can no longer be silent. Careful attention to developing patterns of rhetoric and analyzing potential audiences while in theological education might just help equip current and future ministers of the church with the skills necessary to help the church not only become relevant in cultural conversations but also transformative. If we heed this call to prophetic, reconciliatory rhetoric, perhaps we have a chance to elevate our culture of dialogue within the contemporary world in a way that can mend some rifts in the human community and lead toward unity and redemption.

7. For more insight, read the chapter "Writing Creatively."

3

Writing for the Ear

Karyn L. Wiseman

Writing can be both thrilling and challenging, joyful and difficult. Whatever your purpose is for writing, the task of writing itself can be both enriching and infuriating. Whatever reason brings you to the task, thinking intentionally about writing is important though far from easy.

Some of us write for a living. Some of us write for fun. Many of us write for school or continuing education. Still others write as a hobby. In theological education, writing is a regular—even ubiquitous—part of your life. Whether that means writing an academic paper, a personal theological statement, ordination paperwork, sermons, or church newsletter articles, writing is a key element of ministry and theological education. Most of these writing projects are crafted to be read on paper or on a screen. That is, our prevailing assumption is that these writing projects will be *read*.

However, in seminary, in theological education, and in ministry, another type of writing is absolutely necessary—writing for the ear, writing that will be *heard* more than *read*. This type of writing is an important part of ministry but is also not always considered purposefully. I was lucky. I saw this type of engagement with the task of writing from an early age.

I grew up watching my father, a United Methodist pastor, write out his sermons longhand on a yellow legal pad at his desk or at the kitchen table. Any quotations he found he would write out or copy and tape on the yellow legal pad. He would also write out exegesis notes from his biblical research on the passage of the day, and he would sketch out stories he was considering using for the sermon. Over the next few days, I would see him cut and paste the items from his yellow pad in a variety of formations on new pages of a different yellow legal pad. It was his process. (It is the equivalent of the copy and paste method most of us use with word processing programs today.) While doing all this, my dad would practice the pieces in his head as he walked back and forth to the office or as he worked around the house.

When I would ask him what he was doing, he would respond that he was "making a sermon" out of his notes. He was crafting the written word all through the week. I was watching the creative writing process at work right before my eyes.

But he was not just writing a document. He was also intentionally crafting a spoken-word event. There is a difference between writing to be read and writing to be heard. I can sit and craft a speech or lecture to be given on an academic paper or topic and write to my heart's content. I can wordsmith the sentences and paragraphs to make sure they are perfected in every way possible.[1] I can edit until the cows come home. I can craft a "perfect" or near-perfect read.

---

1. *Wordsmithing* is a word introduced to me by Leonard I. Sweet when I was his teaching and research assistant at Drew Theological Seminary while doing my PhD in the graduate school. It means twisting and turning, perfecting and refining one's written work as a blacksmith does with metals. The intent of wordsmithing is to craft the most perfect sentences and paragraphs

But that is not what my dad was doing.

He was an English major in college, and he knew the difference between spoken-word writing and written-word writing. And it made all the difference in his preaching. He sounded relational, connected, and engaging well before those qualities started showing up regularly in appointment and call documents for churches seeking new pastoral leadership.

What I learned from my dad has stuck with me for all these years. I do not write sermons to be read. I write them to be spoken. And that makes all the difference for the listener.

Theological Writing for the Ear

No matter the assignment, people come to the task of writing about theology differently than other types of writing. Whether writing for a theology class, designing a vacation Bible school curriculum, creating a prayer for a youth worship service, writing an article for a church newsletter, or crafting a Sunday sermon, writing theologically is an indispensable part of the task of people in seminary, people in ministry, and those living and working in collaboration with faith communities.

Coming to the task of theological writing means first determining what it is you believe—about God, about the Bible, about life, about humanity, about sin, about faith. Sometimes as we write, we are still (maybe even always) forming our specific faith expressions and belief systems. In the midst of the assignment, we often find meaning and clarity through the very act of writing. At times, we are given the assignment to write a more technical paper for a history course or an exegetical examination of a biblical passage. In such assignments,

possible. Some who wordsmith can become so focused on the perfecting of their written work that they ignore the content of their compositions.

our beliefs do not have to be articulated in the same ways as they do in other theological writing assignments. These types of writing can be experienced differently from theological or reflective writing in a number of ways. But first and foremost, these papers are typically crafted as documents to be read by an instructor and not by many others. These papers need to be technically accurate, have clear and concise content, and be grammatically well crafted. After all, we do want a good grade on these papers.

Theological writing is thus imperative for anyone thinking about a career in ministry or entering seminary. Engaging in the process of theological learning means that many of these writing assignments are going to be historical, technical, and academic. That is a given.

But not all writing needs to be written for the purpose of reading, which is the more normative writing practice in theological school. We also have to prepare to write for the ear—writing for the listener and with hearing as the primary driver. This is a rather different way of engaging the writing process.

This type of writing must be done with great intentionality and purpose. Just as my father did many years ago, I sit down to craft a sermon with my exegetical materials, notes, and a yellow legal pad (in this approach, I am kind of old school, but I also do this electronically more and more often). I begin with the biblical text and read it in a number of different translations. I do exegetical work from commentaries and online resources. Then, I begin to craft a spoken-word document by paying purposeful and intentional attention to the phrasing of my sentences. I do this not to wordsmith them technically and grammatically but to create phrases and descriptive images that will, I hope, inspire, encourage, challenge, and educate my listeners.

And I am doing all this with an ear toward hearing.

When artists craft their wares, they pay particular attention to the ways they are inspired and also to the ways their creations are possibly going to be seen, heard, or experienced. They do not let those who will receive their works determine the complete outcome, but they do listen to the opinions, interests, and needs of others. They pay attention to how their work will be transmitted and how it will potentially be received by those who view their paintings, read their poetry, gaze at their photos or sculptures, or witness their dances. They may or may not totally take into account what they believe others might need or want, but they often are intentional about how and if they choose to incorporate these ideas. Paying attention to this process of discernment is important for the writer who is writing with the listener in mind.

Writing for the ear means paying attention to the act of listening as well as writing and speaking. How will this idea be heard in my particular context? How might I phrase this concept for the best possible hearing? What are the colloquial or regional phrases I need to employ? Are there issues in my community of faith that need to be handled carefully or that I should engage in more cautiously? How might these issues be heard in my context?

Being sensitive to one's context, regardless of the purpose and intent of the task, is important. In real estate, the motto is, "Location, location, location." In ministry and preaching, the motto is, "Context, context, context." You must be conscious of the issues related to the place where you are ministering. Not doing so means ignoring the specifics of your particular audience, their experiences, and the contextual needs of the particular time to which you are speaking. In the act of writing, you need to write well and craft your words to be listened to by a particular audience, at a particular time, in a particular place, and for a particular moment in time. This is important for all writing, but it is especially true for oral events.

I grew up listening to preaching. I was trained as a preacher. I have a PhD in homiletics and teach preaching in seminary. I have preached sermons for more than twenty years. All my experience has taught me over and over again that writing for the ear, especially for preaching, is a different kind of writing than almost any other genre.

To Be Clear about Writing for the Ear

First, writing for the ear needs to be more conversational and more concerned with hearing. At least, it should be. It isn't always. And that is one common problem with many sermons today. Make sure your writing is conversational in nature, utilizing a tone of voice in the writing that is, at the very least, similar to the tone and cadence of your typical speaking rhythm. Make sure the listener is the focus of your writing as you craft your sermons, Bible studies, or prayers.

Many moments in theological education require writing for the ear. You might be working on a sermon. You might be crafting new liturgies for a specific life event or community transition. You might be creating a prayer for baptism. In any case, your writing should rely on more conversational tones and more hearing-oriented language.

Writing for the ear means thinking about language intentionally. How might you tell this story at the dinner table or to a friend at a coffee shop? What would the tone of voice sound like if you were talking with a group about this information or idea? Where would you stand and how would you use the volume, inflection, and pace of your voice in that conversation?

Think about writing more for conversation and dialogue than for accuracy of grammar and structure. Think about crafting a script to be spoken rather than an academic paper to be read. Think about writing a story or narrative that is plot and character driven.

Second, preaching and teaching require a clear understanding of the intended audience. Who are they? What do they like to do in their spare time? What sports teams in the area do they root for? What types of music do they listen to outside of church? What TV shows and movies do they watch? What books are they reading? What is their theology of humanity? That is, do they think of people as sinners, saints, or some combination of the two? What types of worship do they prefer? What level of education do most of them have? What are their political and theological leanings?

Knowing your context changes how you write. Knowing your context changes how you understand the task of preaching and teaching. Knowing your context changes how you construct spoken encounters with God, the word, and the people to whom you write.

When you write for the ear, think about your target audience. It may very well be a moving target with constant changes in the intended listener pool you may be addressing, but picture one or two persons to whom you will be speaking. Congregations and communities of faith are constantly changing. New people are welcomed. Children and youth grow and change. Some move away. Plus, news of war and tragedy and loss are always with us. So that target audience will be different because they and you and the world are always changing. Despite this, you still need to think about who they are, how they live their lives, what interests they have, and what they need to hear as you write for this moment in time. This kind of directed writing will go a long way to making writing for the ear an intentional practice in your ministry toolbox.

Third, it is pivotal for the writer to understand clearly what the text and context are and to discern how that text and context lead the writer to craft a document to speak to this particular moment in time. Many a speech, sermon, or lesson has gone off the rails for listeners because the speaker lost track of what it was they were trying to say and to whom. Sometimes that happens in the spur of the moment during the speaking, but too often it happens during the crafting phase because the writer lacks focus. What is the one thing you want to communicate?

In writing for the ear, think about the theme or focus of what it is you want to convey. What specifically do you want to present? Make sure you do not have multiple foci in your crafting of this word. You need to have absolute clarity about your intention. If someone asked you what your sermon or Bible study was about, could you answer him or her in one short, concise sentence? If you can, you likely have a pretty clear focus or theme. If you can't, then perhaps your writing has too many themes or an unclear purpose. Work at being as direct and focused as you can be. Too many different directions in one sermon, study, or prayer will make it hard for you to keep track of your intention, and it will make it difficult for your listeners to keep track of what you are saying.

Fourth, one of the best practices of writing for the ear is to keep the writing more narrative and plot driven. This type of writing is often easier to craft and is certainly often more engaging. It is also easier to listen to and follow in a speaking event.

Think of a story you enjoy telling about your life, one you would tell around the family dining table. It might be an exciting vacation story, a funny or absurd work experience, a fond memory from childhood, a story about a favorite uncle taking you fishing, or the birth story of your child.

Remember and think about the setting and the characters. Consider the chronology of the story. What happened in the story first, second, third? Ponder where the action took place. Was it a new place or someplace familiar? Imagine the location in your mind. See the images in color. What are the primary colors, shapes, and images? What words come to mind to describe the scene? What language will you need to employ to describe the characters? What are the people in your story like? Are they kind, empathetic, goofy, funny, lighthearted, sullen, temperamental, happy? How do they drive the action of the story forward? What descriptions will you need to include to help others understand these characters? Should you tell the story in chronological order or mix things up a bit? What method of telling this story will bring listeners into it in the best ways possible?

Could you tell this story without writing it out? Of course you could.

Could you tell this story without reading it aloud from a manuscript? Of course you could.

And that is the primary point of writing for the ear. People hearing story and narrative want to be enveloped by the words and images. They want descriptive language that takes them to a different place and time. They want imagery and plot that entice the imagination. They do not want to be lulled to sleep while someone reads a story about their own life.

A few years ago, my family visited a church for a baptism. During the sermon, a pastor rose to the pulpit, pulled her sermon pages out with a flourish, and started reading a story about her family's recent vacation. They had been canoeing, and their boat had flipped over. The gist of the story was that a water snake had crawled into the boat overnight and the preacher's teenage son saw it, jumped up, and flipped the canoe over. Everyone wound up in the water, scared of the snake, and frantically keeping an eye out for it while trying to grasp all their belongings before everything floated away. The son was sixteen years old and over six foot four, so the whole family cracked up that he was the one who squealed like a baby when he saw the snake.

The story was cute and the point she made using the story was valid, relevant to the text, and contextually interesting. But sitting right in front of my family were two little old ladies (they described themselves that way when we entered that morning). They had been listening to the pastor read the story—word for word—from her sermon manuscript. When the story was finished, one leaned over to the other and said, "Her memory is worse than ours. Didn't that just happen to them?"

These two women knew that the story, while entertaining and fun, lacked something. Their ears liked the content they heard; they did not, however, relate to *how* it was told to them. The language the pastor used to describe things sounded academic and clinical. It was disconnected from her lived reality. The punch lines were stepped on without the appropriate pauses and vocal inflections. The story was not written in a conversational tone. I have no idea if the preacher always preaches this way or if this was just a bad week.

The intentionality and focus on listening and the listener as part of the writing task was clearly not part of that sermon. We knew it. And I think she knew it as well. Because of that, her story did not seem genuine or authentic. It seemed wooden and detached. And she clearly had not rehearsed it enough to know it by heart.

Why didn't she trust her memory to tell that story? Why didn't she lead with the personal narrative from her memory in a language that was conversational and relaxed? I am not sure. Some preachers just do not trust their memories. Others do not put in the necessary time to practice and memorize their stories to the point of learning them completely. Some are afraid to tell a story from memory for fear that they might leave an integral step out of the story. Still others are so committed to precise language and wordsmithing their document that letting go of any control in the process is not possible for them.

Working in a way that writing becomes a dialogue between writer and reader is important. But in writing for the ear, the dialogue process and the dialogue partners are somewhat different from those in writing for reading. The dialogue is directed between the speaker and the listener. The partners are collaborating on the hearing by enriching the language, imagery, and context as they speak and listen. It is an active experience, rather than the typical passive-receptor experience of reading a paper written for reading.

Writing for the ear in seminary or theological education is an essential part of your education and formation. Writing for the ear is writing dialogue. Writing for the ear is writing with context in mind. Writing for the ear is crafting a document to be heard rather than read. Writing for the ear is about connection and engagement. Writing for the ear is about creativity and conversation.

Yes, writing for the ear may take a little bit more time and intentionality, but it is so worth the effort. Your listeners will appreciate your writing for the ear because you are writing with them in mind. You will be more engaging and relevant because you are taking the time and making the effort to write in a way that honors who your listeners are. Because your words will be more effective when they are written for their actual intention, the impact they have will be more profound. So take the time to write for the ear. It will make a huge difference.

4

Writing Briefly

Shively T. J. Smith

> For our speech will never become forcible and energetic unless
> it acquires strength from great practice in writing.
>   –Quintilian, *Institutes of Oratory*, 10.1.2[1]

Who doesn't want to speak with force and energy?

As seminarians, I suspect you, like Quintilian, want to preach,
teach, *and* write with impact and vigor. Quintilian was a first-century
Roman rhetorician who lived in Rome during the time the New
Testament writings were being composed and the Christian
movement emerging. He gained notoriety for his moving speeches
and written rhetorical guidelines. Yet, even he had to admit the truth:
force and energy come with practice.

---

1. Translation taken from Quintilian, *Quintilian on the Teaching of Speaking and Writing:
Translations from Books One, Two, and Ten of the Institutio Oratoria,* ed. James Jerome Murphy
(Carbondale and Edwardville: Southern Illinois University Press, 1987), 125.

Quintilian suggests that oral speech develops persuasiveness through the practice of writing, not more speech making. As such, we acquire forceful and energetic speech only after we have practiced writing forcefully and energetically. What a task this is, especially when one criterion of our communication is to be brief.

Although this chapter is named "Writing Briefly," an equally appropriate title could be "Writing Plainly." The reason is because to be brief and not plain often means the theological perspectives we share are undeveloped, fragmented, or buried under unnecessary statements and information. When writing theology briefly, we want to make it plain, compelling, *and* comprehensible to all our readers. From our professors to members of our Bible study at the women's prison, we want people to understand what we are saying and be compelled to action. Even though it may be brief, we, nonetheless, want our writing to do exactly what Quintilian proposes: to communicate with force and energy.

For many seminarians, graduate school is a step toward lifelong work in pastoral ministries, civic service, or social justice. This means that the theological writing and reflection done in seminary is not just a means to an end (that is, a diploma) but the beginning of our life's work. For many of us, our future is full of writing opportunities and requirements. We will write weekly sermons. We will write Bible studies. We will write church newsletters and inspirational words for our Sunday bulletins. We will write and shape liturgies for Christian holidays such as Ash Wednesday, Advent, and Pentecost. We will write comforting words to those wrestling with loss and grief. We will write inspirational words to high school graduates headed off to college and launching into the world with hopes, dreams, and enthusiasm. We will write grant proposals for our next nonprofit endeavor.

Most of the time, all this writing requires brief and plain speech. Yet, we hope that our brevity and our directness can impact our readers. We hope it compels our readers to be more introspective, more faithful, more loving. We hope that even in short form, we can inspire, instruct, direct, and persuade. As a seminarian, you have a variety of theologies at your disposal, personal experiences to recall, theological references to consult, and passionate convictions to express. How can you write theology briefly and plainly when you have all that whirling around in your mind and troubling your soul?

The skill of writing briefly and plainly becomes easier the more we do it and the more we spend time prayerfully and faithfully thinking about what our theological voice sounds like in written form. As you think about what it means to write briefly, it is helpful to ask the question, what might writing briefly and plainly look like in practice? Drawing insights from other experienced writers as well as the Christian Scriptures, I offer four strategies to enhance your ability to write briefly.

Go Long, Not Short, and Make a Mess

One common misconception about good theological writing is that it has to be long, dense, and—quite frankly—boring. Although engaging and highly thought provoking, who really wants to cuddle up at night and read Karl Barth's *Church Dogmatics*? The prose, while powerful, tends to be long, obscure, and cryptic. Yet, good theological writing can be brief and still have genuine impact and persuasive appeal. The trick is not to start writing with brevity and cohesion as your immediate goal.

One of my favorite writers, Anne Lamott, makes a similar point about the writing process. She says, "The first draft is the child's draft, where you let it all pour out and then let it romp all over the place, knowing that no one is going to see it and that you can shape it later."[2]

A fundamental misstep to avoid in writing theology in short form is to begin with the goal of writing briefly. Such a lofty endeavor can stunt creativity. Your first draft does not have to have force, energy, and cohesion. Your first draft should be what Lamott calls a "child's draft." It should be long, verbose, and jumbled. Interrogative words—such as why, where, how, when, who—should be at work. Your ideas should be piled one on top of the other. There may be some clarity, some direction, but not necessarily succinctness. It should be full of possible writing directions, with no track fully developed. Just possibilities.

What would happen if you started writing with the express intention of making a mess? Instead of focusing on crafting a polished and coherent theological magnum opus, what if you shifted your focus to writing in order to get what is in your mind out with all its incoherence, incomplete sentences, colloquialisms, and fragmented thoughts? What if writing plainly started with diversity, not uniformity?

I often make this exact point to my students in my Introduction to New Testament Gospels class. Our New Testament canon does not contain just one harmonious story about Jesus but four distinct stories. At times, these stories are similar, and the storylines agree, especially in their narration of Jesus' final week. Other moments, the stories are different, even contradictory. For instance, all four Gospels have a version of Jesus cleansing the temple. But whereas in the Gospel of John it occurs at the beginning of Jesus' ministry (John 2:13-25), in the other Gospels it occurs near the end of his ministry, leading up to his crucifixion (Matt. 21:12-17; Mark 11:15-19; Luke

2. Anne Lamott, *Bird By Bird: Some Instructions on Writing and Life* (New York: Anchor Books, 1995), 22.

19:45-46). Here, we encounter the same event but different points of view about what it means and its significance and place in the context of Jesus' ministry. These are four perspectives, four proclamations, and four opportunities to think about Jesus' life and ministry. All are Scripture and offer viable possibilities, but at any given moment, you can explore only one in depth.

In similar fashion, we write at length to get all the possibilities out on paper, to examine complex questions from many different angles. It is so easy to be a long-winded writer and to get lost in our own theological reflections. Instead of stifling that impulse, we should embrace it as an important start in our writing process. Oftentimes, it is only after pages and pages of discourse that we arrive at a point that makes sense and offers a prospective train of thought worth following. Rarely does theological writing start out clear, concise, and coherent in the child's draft. It takes time. You have to write yourself into understanding and then take more time to make your perspective comprehensible to others. You have to give yourself permission to write your way into clarity and to start the process by making a mess.

Write When Led by the Spirit . . . and When Not

Discipline yourself to write as the spirit hits you, so to speak. When ideas, insights, perspectives start running through your head, stop what you are doing and jot them down. Jump out of the shower and scribble what is in your head on some paper. If you are walking across campus, use your voice recorder on your phone and dictate what is in your head and transcribe later—just not too much later. You can build, develop, and clarify when you have more dedicated time.

The first task in writing anything is just to write. And then write some more. Many seminarians see their final papers and projects as an end rather than a beginning. Students often just want to know their final grade, and they discard all the writing they have done. However, much of that writing represents a good starting point for the sermons, liturgies, and Bible studies you will have to produce in the near future. For instance, the theological paper you wrote exploring the history of the Christian calendar or the exegesis paper on Matthew's version of Jesus' death on the cross are excellent starting points to keep you writing.

Therefore, your seminary work offers you an opportunity to continue to write and build your written portfolio. You just have to make it your discipline to expand it. You have to continue to write, even if you are just making a mess.

Be Selective

Did you know that the writer of Mark tells us he knows more than he writes in his Gospel? Throughout the Gospel are summaries of Jesus' teachings and activities. For instance, Mark 1:34 says Jesus "cured many who were sick with various diseases, and cast out many demons." Similarly, Mark 4:33 says, "With many such parables he spoke the word to them." Although Mark provides specific details about some of Jesus' healings, exorcisms, and parables, they appear to be only a fraction of the data set Mark had available to him. Mark made concrete decisions about what to include and what to exclude.

Therefore, one key to the brevity and directness of Mark's Gospel is that he did not include everything. He shared what he thought would have the greatest impact in his account of Jesus. He gave the details that he thought made the point he wanted to make, which was to share that the good news of Jesus Christ is that he is the Son of God (Mark 1:1).

We should probably take some lessons on the recipe for writing briefly and plainly from this Gospel writer. First, take the guesswork out of your main point. You do not have the space or room to take your readers on a mystery journey. In fact, your professors and parishioners are not interested in surprise endings. Tell your surprise up front—plainly.

Then, be selective. You do not have the space to share every piece of evidence in support of your claim and position, so don't. Pick those pieces of evidence that best support your position. From your extended drafts, pick those sections that are eloquent and most rhetorically persuasive. Communicate in written form those pieces that most directly help you make your point.

Once you have a good sense about the content of your free writing and you have identified potential content worth keeping, create an entirely new document with just that content. Try to string sections together that you think could potentially fit well with some revision. Try out different organizational patterns and structures. Then, reverse outline your outcome.

Reverse outlining is a method in which you write first, outline second. Instead of telling the body of your writing how it should flow and what the content should do, you let your free writing and revision tell you what is emerging from the mire of words and ideas. As the proverbial saying goes, "And a little child shall lead them."[3] Let your child's draft tell you what you want to discuss.

Like formal outlines, your reverse outline can be linear with a header topic and subordinate points in which you identify the topic sentences of each paragraph. Alternatively, your reverse outline could be a mind map of sorts where you put the main topic in a bubble with

---

3. This popular axiom comes from Isaiah 11:6, which is actually a discussion about the day of the Lord in which peace and harmony will be restored to all creation. This means even wolves, lambs, leopards, cobras, and children will live in harmony with one another.

lines extending out to create another bubble or subordinate point. Your aim at this point is to discern the logic and direction of your writing. You are trying to find the flow of thought or speech pattern and make a decision on whether that is where you want to head in your writing.

After all, the goal in this specific task is not to write long but to write with a clear point and direction in mind. To write briefly and plainly is to write with clarity and aim. You need to know the one or two points you want to make and try to make those points with force and energy.

Writing to Translate

Few beginning seminary students are skilled writers of formal theological reflection essays or exegetical papers, but many are accustomed to producing short writing pieces. Perhaps you come to seminary having already written for the church bulletin or newsletters. Maybe you have crafted and conducted Bible studies. You might have outlined and presented a sermon or two. In short, you may have started seminary accustomed to writing briefly.

The challenge facing you is not how to resume your brief writing stints but how to bring all that you have learned to those tasks. You will graduate from seminary with a lot of information you could share. The information you have learned, the questions you have contemplated, the research you have conducted, and the experiences you have had are important for the life and future of the church. Although the short writing tasks you have in church or the communities you serve have not changed, you will have changed as you move through seminary.

Many seminarians decide that the theological writing they did in theology school has no place in their actual ministerial contexts.

They think, "No one will understand Karl Barth." Or, "The Synoptic problem will enrage my senior members and confuse the new members." But this is a misconception. Good translation makes clear to audiences outside seminary the usefulness of theological writing and engagement. Translation can render the most dense and difficult theological concepts comprehensible to lay audiences. It fosters the opportunity for them to connect to the information in real, concrete ways.

You have a responsibility to make that process of faithful and critical engagement available in your ministerial settings and service communities. You are duty bound to translate what you have learned into comprehensive pieces that nonacademics and nonseminarians can process. How do you enrich your short writing assignments with the critical knowledge and insight now available to you? That is the question and the challenge before you.

The audience for theological writing shifts from moment to moment and context to context. One difficulty in theological writing is making the shift from formal and professional theological audiences to a lay readership. One way of writing theology plainly is identifying your audience. After I write at length and make a mess, I am still slated with the task of shaping and structuring my writing into a mode of communication or proclamation that makes sense to a specific audience. My rhetorical end is to say something that makes sense and has an impact on a particular public. Theologian David Tracy specifies three publics or audiences for theological writing: academic context and theological school, the ministerial context and church, and wider society.[4]

---

4. David Tracy, *The Analogical Imagination: Christian Theology and the Culture of Pluralism* (New York: Crossroad, 1981), 31, referenced in Lucretia B. Yaghjian, *Writing Theology Well* (New York: Continuum, 2006), 15.

An important starting point in translation is naming your receptor language. This is no less true in writing theology. Writing theology plainly is not just about mechanics. It is about translating the difficult and obscure into the comprehensible and simple. How do you make the complex graspable? That is the work of the seminarian when approaching audiences that are not academics. That is critical for anyone going into ministry. Outside seminary, you are expected to deliver to nonacademic audiences concise, clear, and precise speech.

Much of seminary is spent developing only one mode of communication and only talking or theorizing about the rest. For most of us, by the time we finish seminary, we have become proficient academic writers of exegetical papers and theological reflection essays. The mystery for many of us is how to translate that mode of communication into a mode of proclamation that our ministerial contexts and wider society can understand and appreciate. How do we take those exegetical papers and turn them into forceful, energetic, and compelling sermons? Can we transform our academic writing into modes of communication that satisfy an audience other than our professors and fellow seminarians?

Learning to write theology briefly and plainly involves considering both the obscure and the simple. It includes naming the complex while simultaneously describing it in everyday terms. It is a transliteration of sorts, substituting the complex technical jargon of the academy with the common vernacular of the people with whom you actually interact on a daily basis. The trick is to force yourself to define and nuance theological terminology. Writing plainly sometimes means using more words. It is opting for the many over the one because the latter is just not enough to be forceful and comprehensible.

Take, for example, calling. In ministerial settings, especially many mainline ordination processes, the language of calling is commonplace. Yet, many seminarians during their ordination process find that communicating their understanding of call and their personal call experience is difficult—even gut wrenching. Why? Much of the anxiety certainly is related to the situation and audience—members of the ordination board judge your vocational trajectory and ministerial future. However, another layer of this anxiety is related to the meaning of call. What do they think call means? Is that the same as your thoughts and does that correspond with your experience? The word *call* is not enough. We have to spend time defining what we mean, naming call as the work we do for God on behalf of God's people.

Another example is the youth pastor who wants to talk about call. She may find that starting with the sixteenth-century German Reformer Martin Luther's definition of call, although provocative, may not be the most productive opener for a Wednesday night youth group.[5] Yet, she does not have to discard altogether Luther's long and dense theological statement. She just has to spend some time exploring how to present it in digestible pieces. Theological writing is about inquiry and journeying as much as it is about making propositions and statements. It can help youth and adults learn what their voices sound like as inquisitors and respondents. It should compel us to define our terms and understanding.

In addition to defining terms, another approach to translation is substitution and paraphrasing. Sometimes, our best points are made

---

5. "In a sermon on Christian liberty, Luther says, 'What you do in your house is worth as much as if you did it up in Heaven for our Lord God. For what we do in our calling here on earth in accordance with His word and command He counts as if were done in heaven for Him. . . . In whatever calling God has placed you do not abandon it when you become a Christian. If you are a servant, a maid, a workman, a master, a housewife, a mayor, a prince, do whatever your position demands. For it does not interfere with your Christian faith and you can serve God rightly in any vocation. . . . Therefore we should accustom ourselves to think of our position and work as sacred and well-pleasing to God, not on its own account, but because of the word and the faith from which our obedience flows.'" Arthur Cushman McGiffert, *Martin Luther: The Man and His Work* (New York: The Century Company, 1911), 177.

with a picture. Here, I am not referring just to actual photographs or paintings. We can draw word pictures that stick in the minds and stir the spirits of readers just as powerfully as any visual image. Sometimes, a well-chosen metaphor has more force and energy than anything else we can say.

Again, we follow the lead of the New Testament canon. The Bible is replete with word pictures or metaphors. How many times have we heard Paul's soliloquy on love in 1 Corinthians and imagined the jarring clang of an out-of-tune cymbal? Or who doesn't cringe from the mind picture drawn from Jesus calling his opponents whitewashed tombs and a brood of vipers? Or who doesn't feel empathy for the prodigal son contemplating eating from the pigs' trough? Opting to describe the picture, instead of elaborating the concept, can have more impact. It can make your point clearer and faster. Oftentimes, it even sharpens your understanding of a concept.

Conclusion

Writing theology briefly is about being willing to make a mess first. We start the journey of writing theology not knowing where we are going. Understanding happens once we faithfully take our journey reading and discussing, engaging in class and reviewing notes. Good written theology happens when we write and rewrite our theological reflections, positions, and insights in different ways for different audiences and then we let it go. Author Kathleen Norris says, "Writing a sermon is like any other form of writing, because I have to settle for doing the best I can, and then let it go."[6] Writing briefly and plainly entails making our best effort to translate our thoughts and make them comprehensible to other audiences.

6. Kathleen Norris, *Amazing Grace: A Vocabulary of Faith* (New York: Riverhead Books, 1998), 181.

Writing briefly and plainly happens at the end, not the beginning. We know we have done it when we can boldly, like the writer of the Gospel of Mark, admit there were more stories we could have told. However, for the sake of this particular moment and written artifact, we are satisfied that those pieces we shared made our message most clear and plain. Writing theology briefly is about looking at the pieces left on the table and saying, "I still made a complete picture even without them." And if we are really lucky, we may see that those pieces left on the table could make another picture that also rings true with force and energy.

5

Writing Creatively

Angela Yarber

> In beginning was the word and the word became God and the
> word was God.
>> —Gospel of John 1:1

> God called forth . . . and it became . . . and it was good.
>> —Genesis 1:3-4 creation narrative

Who: The Creative Theology of Others

Creative words and creative potential burst the world into being, according to the theology of the creation narratives of the opening chapters of Genesis. In John, Jesus was and is and becomes the Word. With words, God calls forth life and trees, stars and sunsets, oceans and rivers, animals and humanity. Color, design, beauty, creativity, and wonder are encapsulated—as best they can be—in words. And as best we can, we use our finite words to capture the infinite.

Theology—faith seeking understanding—is most often articulated in language, words, sentences, grammar, structure, paragraphs, papers, and books. As a professional artist and dancer, I know and believe that theology is not limited to words alone. I also know that not many seminaries or churches, denominational bodies or ordination councils, even fellow people of faith really grasp theology via painting or dance. But most of us—both those who describe ourselves as creative and those who do not—typically use words and language to describe our faith and theology. We say it or write it.

The task of this book is to grapple with writing theologically. And my task is to discuss the power of creativity in our theological writing. So, I begin where any artist, preacher, and scholar considering a creative approach to theological writing would begin: in the Upper Paleolithic period, particularly the Magdalenian era.

Naturally.

The Upper Paleolithic era: eighteen thousand to eleven thousand years ago. Some of our earliest information about the development of humankind, worship, perhaps even theology comes from Upper Paleolithic cave art. Even if you're not an art historian, you're probably more familiar with the artwork than you think: Venus figures, bison, hands outlined in spit-painting color pigments. Spit painting is when the artists breathe life into cold stone by blowing color pigments out of the mouth and onto the massive rock canvas. Human spirit inhabits dry stone.[1]

What is most fascinating about many of these works of art from the Magdalenian period of the Upper Paleolithic is their location. And

---

1. For more on the role of the sacred in Upper Paleolithic cave art, see Margaret Conkey, "New Approaches in the Search for Meaning? A Review of Research in 'Paleolithic Art,'" *Journal of Field Archaeology* 14 (1987): 413–30; John Halverson, "Paleolithic Art and Cognition," *The Journal of Psychology* 126 (1991): 221–36; Michael Barton, G. A. Clark, and Allison Cohen, "Art as Information: Explaining Upper Paleolithic Art in Western Europe," *World Archaeology* 26 (1994): 185–207; and Alejandro García-Rivera, *A Wounded Innocence: Sketches for a Theology of Art* (Collegeville, MN: Liturgical, 2003).

I don't mean Europe or Africa. Rather, I mean the locations within caves. Many of these caves have small, womb-like openings where people once crawled on bellies with only the light of candles to find hidden caverns large enough, worthy enough, and sacred enough for their thoughtful and spirit-filled paintings. It was a treacherous journey toward the infinite, much like the journey of faith and the task of a creative theology.

Most of these paintings are found in open areas within the caves, areas with the highest resonance for singing and chanting. According to ethnomusicologists, these prehistoric artists were essentially looking for the best acoustics, a sacred space worthy enough for their songs. Even more interesting, many of these Magdalenian paintings are not only on display in high resonance areas with the best space for singing but some also have heel prints located in front of the paintings, heel prints dug into dirt and preserved by a ritual spinning movement, similar to that of the Mevlevi Order or the whirling dervishes of Sufism. The paintings were places of singing and dancing.

Phenomenologists and other religious scholars often purport that the assemblage of womb-like cave openings, the belly-to-ground journey to reach the high resonance areas, the paintings, the singing, the chanting, and the dancing indicates nothing less than a prehistoric sanctuary for worship. Creative theology: the arts ritually colliding in a sacred sanctuary of song. Who would have known that before we created an alphabet, before we domesticated animals or agriculture, before cities and commerce and temples and museums and concert halls arose, before we crafted cathedrals that mimic those same womb-like cave openings, our ancient ancestors danced their way, painted their way, sang their way toward the ultimate, the holy, the divine. Not just in song. Not just in visual arts. Not just in dance. But in all the arts enfolding and interconnecting creatively and ritually in a manner that is nothing short of sacred.

Theology, from its very outset, was an exercise in creative imagination.

When we look at our history, the development of humankind and of the church universal, we are connected through the arts. The aesthetic bridges the vast chasm between antiquity and modernity. The arts are our clues into the history of the sacred. Ancient jewelry, sculptures, frescos, mosaics, poetry, calligraphy, and architecture give us tiny glimpses into what had value in years past.

The new archeological discoveries of carved dancers enveloping temple pillars from more than eleven thousand years ago at Göbekli Tepe in southern Turkey confirm that our dancing bodies have been a vital part of worship for centuries. Crumbling mosaics, carvings, and statues remind us that the arts—painting, assemblage, sculpture—predate our holy books and written doctrines. And the deep, brooding, ancient chanting in those high resonance caves is nothing short of a musical miracle that reminds us of the never-ending power of song to carry our prayers toward the holy. We need look no further than the Psalms to see how imaginative words were written or sung as a way of expressing prayer, lament, and praise, not to mention the countless church mothers and fathers who tapped into their creative spirits by penning poetry and prose as a way of connecting to the holy.

Music, art, dance, and creative writing are in our bones. They have been even before recorded history. They have been throughout the Scriptures. And it will continue to be so—I am convinced—because creativity does something theological.

And from here is where we could plow through Scripture and history, highlighting the places where creativity has played a prominent role in theology. We could talk about how the Hebrew

Bible actually uses ten verb forms for our one English word *dance*. We could talk about how we find dancers celebrating, lamenting, alluring, praising, greeting, and grieving throughout the Bible: Miriam, Jephthah's daughter, David, the psalmist, the Shulamite, Judith, Salome, and even Jesus in the apocryphal Acts of John.[2]

We could talk about how many times Scripture admonishes us to sing a new song unto God, to worship with music and song and harp and lyre and drums and horns and strings and pretty much every instrument known in that time. We could talk about the creative spirit endowed in us by our Creator, who magnificently, artistically, intentionally, and creatively stretched a canvas across the heavens and bedabbled it with sparkling paint called stars and fading, glowing, expansive pinks, oranges, fuchsias, indigoes, and golds called sunset. According to Earle Coleman's *Creativity and Spirituality: Bonds between Art and Religion*, "Divine creation is traditionally the model for artistic creativity, because both God and the artist wring order out of chaos, both bring about new universes, and both infuse life or animation into what was lifeless."[3] Creative language. Creative theology. In creating, we become a bit more like God.

Or we could talk about how so many of the church fathers and theologians one learns about in seminary—Gregory of Nyssa, Augustine, Jerome, Martin Luther—wrote about dance as a vital way of worshiping God. It was Basil the Great, after all, who asked, "Could there be anything more blessed than to imitate on earth the ring-dance of the angels and at dawn to raise our voices in prayer and by hymns and song glorify the rising Creator?"[4] We could talk about

---

2. For more on the role of dance in the Bible, see Angela Yarber, *Dance in Scripture: How Biblical Dancers Can Revolutionize Worship Today* (Eugene, OR: Wipf and Stock, 2013).

3. Earle Coleman, *Creativity and Spirituality: Bonds between Art and Religion* (New York: State University of New York Press, 1998), 155.

4. Basil, *Epistle 40*, quoted in Iris Stewart, *Sacred Woman Sacred Dance* (Rochester, NY: Inner Traditions, 2000), 64.

the history of music embedded in the development of the church: Gregorian chants, shape-note singing, organs, and global songs of praise. We could talk about the way much of this music—especially spirituals and gospel—made life more livable for enslaved Africans and how the creative words of this music functioned subversively in the midst of oppression.[5] We could talk about architecture and mosaics, frescos and chapels, stained glass and sculptures, paintings and iconography by the most famous artists in history to little-known folk artists, and how that visual art doesn't merely illustrate the divine, it images the divine. It embodies the divine. It points us to the divine. We could talk about the poetry of Hildegard of Bingen, C. S. Lewis, the Desert Fathers, Ruth Duck, Maya Angelou, or myriad other creative writers who dedicate their artistry to worship and devotion.

Or we could talk about how the arts just do *something*, reach something inside us that our finite language simply can't touch. We could talk about the many times we've tried to pray when our contrived words render us mute or our silent meditation is completely deafening. And when we begin to move our bodies and dance, we know that God has heard our prayers. Or we sit down in front of the piano and our fingers voice our unspoken cries. Or we pick up a paintbrush and when our creative spirit pours onto the canvas, we know that God has witnessed our requests. Or we quiet our own words and instead rely on the creative poetry of the psalmist to utter our prayers. The body, the voice, the paintbrush, the instrument, the pen become conduits for our theology.

Or we could talk about the role of all the arts in every major world religion and how our dances, our music, our creative writing, our visual arts serve as tools, mediums, methods for interfaith dialogue.[6]

---

5. For more on the role of subversion and spirituality in music, see Melva Wilson Costen, *In Spirit and in Truth: The Music of African American Worship* (Louisville, KY: Westminster John Knox, 2004).

We could talk about how when we stop all the dogmatic pontifications and esoteric banter and begin to make art together, sing together, write together, and dance together, then peace might just be possible.

We could talk about all these things: theology, Scripture, history, spirituality, interfaith dialogue, and the vast witness and working of creativity within these pivotal parts of our faiths. We could continue to talk about how others have utilized their creative spirits theologically. Or we could talk about how *you* can utilize your creative spirit theologically. We could talk about how your own theological writing can be creative and how that very creativity can pave the way for justice, peace, and beauty for all humanity, even all creation. We could talk about how artful and creative theological writing has the potential of fulfilling the gospel and creating a revolution.

So, whether you sing, dance, paint, play an instrument, act, or do none of these things, you have creative capacity dwelling within, and this creative potential may just find its best medium to be theological writing. Again, such creative theological writing can spark a revolution.

Why: Your Creative Theology

> The purpose of a writer is to make revolution irresistible.
> —Toni Cade Bambara[7]

---

6. For more on the role of the arts in interfaith dialogue and the way dance functions in world religions, see Angela Yarber, *Embodying the Feminine in the Dances of the World's Religions* (New York: Peter Lang, 2011).

7. Toni Cade Bambara, *This Bridge Called My Back: Writings by Radical Women of Color*, eds. Cherríe Moraga and Gloria Anzaldúa (New York: Kitchen Table, Women of Color Press, 1981), viii.

For those discerning or living a call to ministry, the role of creativity in theological writing cannot be overestimated. For me, a tremendous part of my own calling is to overturn unjust systems of oppression, violence, and exclusion. This is the essence of Jesus' message when he spoke of freeing the oppressed, setting free the prisoners, and proclaiming the favorable year of God in the fourth chapter of the Gospel of Luke. While some may wonder why creativity is important in such a calling (perhaps misunderstanding the arts as merely decorative or peripheral), I find that the goal of aesthetics is to create a more beautiful world, a world where everyone can be inspired and surrounded by beauty. Aesthetics, put most simply, is the study of beauty, and in our case, the theology of beauty. Justice is not attained simply when the hungry are fed horrible processed food or when those without a home are covered by a dank and rickety shelter, for example. Rather, when all have equal access to what is beautiful, delicious, healthy, and inspiring, then justice has come. Our creative theological efforts, inspired by a God who yearns for justice, have the ability to create such a world. Our creative theological efforts, inspired by a God whose grace knows no bounds, make revolution irresistible.

Mary Farrell Bednarowski discusses the power of "lump in the throat" stories to evoke not merely a theology of hope but an aesthetic of hope.[8] What do God and our hopes have to do with the sights, sounds, and experiences that delight us? This aesthetic of hope is the pathway to just beauty, creative living that is sustainable, equal, fair, and peace filled. It is the life Jesus proclaimed during his first sermon in Luke 4. It is the life all theologians are called to proclaim, live, and most important, create. Bednarowski highlights "lump in the throat" stories in the creative writing of several spiritual

8. Mary Farrell Bednarowski, "Lump in the Throat Stories," in *Arts, Theology, and the Church*, ed. Kimberly Vrudny and Wilson Yates (Cleveland: Pilgrim, 2005): 50–70.

memoirs. She defines these stories as *spiritual* in order to point toward creative writing about religious experiences that elicits an emotional and intellectual response, evoking a deep feeling that has affective and aesthetic content, stirring both the head and the heart simultaneously.

We all have such "lump in the throat" stories simmering inside us, and when artfully and creatively communicated in thoughtful writing, these stories can elicit similar responses in others. These theological stories can incite a revolution. *Your* theological stories can incite a revolution.

And yet we too often find that those of us who go through seminary, think theologically, and engage in ministry tend to write about these experiences in a way that is not creative, artful, or theologically sound. Some writers ascribe to a health-and-wealth prosperity gospel in which God "blesses" those who are rich and in good health, claiming that their prayers are answered when illness is cured, when they experience a fortuitous turn in the stock market, or when their favorite sports team is victorious. In doing so, writers damn entire demographics of people who are not afforded the same luxuries or privileges yet who still have deep, abiding faith. For these reasons *New York Times Sunday Book Review* columnist Judith Shulevitz does not like the genre of the spiritual memoir.[9] She claims that most lack artfulness, sound mawkish, and are filled with oracular pronouncements that aim to separate the writer from the reader, rather than engaging the senses, the spirit, and the mind. The task of good theological writing—creative theological writing—is to engage the senses, the spirit, and the mind simultaneously. Each time a theologian writes, she has this opportunity. Each time a preacher pens a sermon, she has this opportunity. And each time a student works on a seminary paper, she has this opportunity. This creative

---

9. See Judith Shulevitz, "In God They Trust, Sort of," *The New York Times Sunday Book Review,* August 25, 2002, 27.

shift in perspective can certainly revolutionize a student's approach to writing required papers in seminary.

How might your attitude, your devotion, and your writing shift if you viewed a writing assignment as a gift? What if your assignments were an opportunity to express creatively your theology in such a way that you may create a lump in your professor's throat rather than merely meet a required deadline on the way to a terminal degree? For when it comes to creative theological writing, such work, such art is never merely an assignment or a deadline. It is a creative opportunity to wonder, worship, marvel, and artfully create a world that is more beautiful and just.

Creative theological writing is a necessary—and life-giving—part of a minister's calling. The question is how? How does one write more creatively, more theologically, more artfully, more justly, more beautifully? How do you write to create revolution?

How: Creating Creative Theology

There is no greater agony than bearing an untold story inside you.

—Maya Angelou[10]

Write.

The first step in becoming a better creative theological writer is simply to write. Poet and author Maya Angelou is correct in asserting that keeping your story inside is an agony. Don't keep your stories, your theologies inside, but write about them. Practice writing about them. And write about them often.

---

10. Maya Angelou, *I Know Why the Caged Bird Sings* (New York: Random House, 1969), 11.

Read good writing. If you want to write creatively, theologically, artfully, or in such a way that you cause a "lump in the throat" of your readers, read writing that creates a lump in your own throat. Read theologians who write beautifully, creatively, and artfully. For example, Catherine Keller, Marcella Althaus-Reid, and Kimerer LaMothe are all stunning theologians who write creatively and beautifully.[11] Read theologians who are creative. Read creative writers who dabble in theology. Maya Angelou, Anne Lamott, Wendell Berry, Alice Walker, Barbara Kingsolver are all creative writers who have mastered the art of language, wordsmiths who can also hold their own theologically even though they may not be trained theologians.[12] Read creative writers who utilize theology. And read good novels that may not deal directly with theology but often and necessarily deal with beauty, pain, ecstasy, grief, passion, and wonder. These things are also deeply theological. Read about them, too.

Proofread what you write. Many writers (including yours truly) often finish penning an essay only to pat themselves on the back, applauding their brilliance, certain that the sheer beauty of their theological writing will create life-altering lumps in the throat of every person whose eyes grace their stunningly written pages. Let's be honest. Usually this is not the case.

11. While the list of their writings is far too long to include in a footnote, a helpful starting point for each author includes Catherine Keller, *Face of the Deep: A Theology of Becoming* (London: Routledge, 2003); Marcella Althaus-Reid, *Indecent Theology: Theological Perversions in Sex, Gender, and Politics* (New York: Routledge, 2000); and Kimerer LaMothe, *Between Dancing and Writing: The Practice of Religious Studies* (New York: Fordham University Press, 2004).
12. The list of their writings is also too long to include in a footnote, but good starting places include Maya Angelou, *I Know Why the Caged Bird Sings* (New York: Random House, 1969); Anne Lamott, *Traveling Mercies: Some Thoughts on Faith* (New York: Pantheon Books, 1999); Alice Walker, *The Color Purple* (New York: Harcourt Brace Jovanovich, 1982); Wendell Berry, *Recollected Essays: 1965–1980* (San Francisco: North Point, 1981); and Barbara Kingsolver, *The Poisonwood Bible* (New York: Harper, 1998).

Once I've proofread a piece of writing, I realize it's filled with typos. Phrases that I thought were well crafted are missing words. Arguments I thought were without flaw are disconnected. Despite my best efforts, there is sometimes a rogue comma splice or misspelled word. If one writes a paper only hours before it is due, catching such errors is nearly impossible. Accordingly, I would add that procrastination rarely leads to good creative theological writing. If you want to create wonder, awe, justice, and beauty, it is best not to wait until 4:00 a.m. when your deadline is at 9:00 a.m. And if you don't have experience with writing and enter seminary or ministry without knowing about grammar, thesis statements, and how to craft an essay, take advantage of the myriad opportunities available at universities and seminaries and online. Invest in a good style guide. Take a creative writing class. Talk to professors, librarians, and other writers to improve your writing. Listen to what they say. Though it may not seem particularly creative or inspiring, grammar and style are the only primary avenues you have for effectively communicating your theological writing. If the grammar and style are not clear, the possibility for that "lump in the throat," that beauty, and therefore that justice is slim. At the same time, however, it is also vital to question oppressive systems that stifle creativity and privilege only those who have had access to ivory towers of so-called correct knowledge. Know that your story, and the theology it represents, is worthy. Do everything you can to communicate that worthwhile story creatively, effectively, and beautifully.

Surround yourself with beauty and create spaces of beauty for others. If Virginia Woolf is correct in asserting that every woman needs a room of her own to stoke her creative spirit, do whatever is in your power to create such a room. This sacred space may be outdoors, on public transportation, in a public library, or in a literal room with a view that causes your jaw to drop in wonder.

I cannot even calculate the creative words written on a screeching, smelly train as it pulsed through the bay. The variety of people, the grandeur of the sprawling bay spilling into the Pacific, and the juxtaposition of urban decay, shipyards, graffiti, and the crippling violence of Oakland poured onto the page. Those putrid seats on the roaring tracks became my room even more so than when I had access to my own office, encased in esoteric books, with a window overlooking magenta crepe myrtles. Choose a space that inspires you. More important, realize your responsibility—as a person called by God—to create such spaces for those who do not have access to such beauty. Create beautiful public spaces that can inspire anyone who walks by and not simply those who can afford an entry fee. Such creation is a theological act.

Write about that.

When: Becoming Creative Theology

Writing saved me from the sin and inconvenience of violence.
—Alice Walker[13]

People of faith have creatively expressed their theology in writing, dance, visual art, music, architecture, and theater before we even coined the term *theology*. As a person of faith, you too have a creative theological story to share. And now is the time to write about it. Now is the time, as Alice Walker has admonished, to write to save your soul from violence. Even more than this, now is the time to harness your creative spirit to shift cycles of violence into cycles of beauty and inspiration.

13. Quoted in *Modern American Women Writers,* ed. Elaine Showalter, Lea Baechler, and A. Walton Litz (New York: Charles Scribner's Sons, 1991), 360.

Write beautifully. Write creatively. Write justly. Write theologically. Write to incite a revolution.

6

Writing Publicly

Grace Ji-Sun Kim

I grew up in the days of the door-to-door encyclopedia salesman. I remember the day when a clean-cut, well-dressed man knocked on our apartment door to sell the twenty-six-volume *World Book Encyclopedia.* We were recent immigrants and could not speak English fluently. We had few worldly possessions and the last thing we needed in our home was a twenty-six-volume encyclopedia.

After the hour-long presentation, during which we flipped through the volumes full of exciting information, my dad said, "No." The salesman looked sad as he packed his sales kit. As he was walking out the door, he gave one last pitch and, suddenly, my dad changed his mind. He bought the whole set. Perhaps the salesman was persuasive. More likely is that my parents had this compulsion that their children needed to know everything there is to know about the world. Maybe it was a bit of both.

In 2014, those twenty-six-volume encyclopedias are long gone. The same is true of most other encyclopedias that once filled the bookshelves of many of my childhood friends' homes. Now, we have everything that we need to know at our fingertips through iPads, computers, cell phones, and other technological gadgets.

We live in a media-saturated society. We no longer need twenty-six-volumes to help us understand the world. Now, all we need is a palm-sized gadget to find the latest news, the juiciest gossip, or up-to-date facts on anything under the sun. We live in a society and culture where information can distract us all day long. How, for example, can some of us work at the computer with both Facebook and e-mail open and stand being pinged every time a friend supplies a comment to one of our most insightful posts? Things we may not want to read or watch seem to appear on our computer screens or on billboards as we drive along the highways. What does it mean for us, and especially for future generations, to live in a media-saturated society with all this information and infomercials thrown at us? We need to be aware of the possibility of becoming overwhelmed by so many words, sounds, and pictures. We can waste hours on social networks, chatting with Facebook friends, checking Twitter, or just surfing the Net. The time can evaporate like the water in an unattended teapot on a flame.

But I think there's an even more pressing concern for us. In a world so consumed by content and digital distractions, how do future leaders of the church participate in these sprawling but important conversations? How do we write publicly, that is, for an audience beyond our immediate circle of influence? And how do we do so in a way that takes the gospel and its impact on our lives seriously? One thing we cannot do is ignore these media. I know of a pastor who less than ten years ago saw no reason whatsoever in learning how to send and receive e-mail. He saw it as a skill like using a fax machine. Why should he bother to learn how to do either when he had secretaries to do that for him? Of course, that pastor grew increasingly distant from members of his congregation who made good use of e-mail. In these times of rapid technological and social change, we must adapt accordingly. In an age of media and information saturation, we too need to participate and immerse ourselves in such places. After all, this is precisely where God and God's Spirit is moving in new and transformative ways today. If we are to be proclaimers of God's good news, then these are the media and places and means by which we can meet the high calling of God to speak a word of grace, joy, and love in a world where we have become too impatient to wait for any of these most precious gifts of God.

Public Lives

We live in an increasingly public world where our lives are more and more lived in and touched by the public. What we wear, what we eat, where we are going, with whom we are hanging around are just some of the things that are becoming increasingly easy for the world to observe. With the rise of social media, our way of being and living can be followed and displayed for the world to see, if we let it.

In this ever-increasingly public life, we need to be aware of how we can most effectively reach out to these diverse audiences. Long gone are the days when staying in touch just meant face-to-face contact or written letters or telephone calls. Today, we can be in touch with people all over the world through landline telephones, Skype, and überconnected mobile devices.

The quantity and breadth of materials accessible online has greatly increased as well. More people are posting their ideas, blogs, comments, pictures, and music than ever before. As such, more and more people are publishing and speaking online to wide audiences previous generations could only dream of.

As we spend more time online and find ourselves in the public sphere more and more, this has important implications for ministers, all of whose callings include trying to reach out to individuals and communities alike with the good news of Jesus Christ. With such a rapid rise of technological amplifiers of our voices, we need to consider how ministers are to communicate with individuals who have not been lifelong church attenders or who are not regular attenders of a church. Furthermore, effective ministry in these changing contexts requires the ability to speak beyond the walls of the church. This is particularly true in a digital age when more people begin their search for God online rather than in our churches.

In such a time as this, how do we write to a public audience, especially to those who may not be predisposed to accept the gospel? It is becoming increasingly important for many ministers and church leaders to write publicly and for a wider audience than just those who sit in our pews. For instance, one essential method of communicating is to show what we do rather than just say what we believe. Churches run soup kitchens every day, all year round. This is newsworthy! That is not only great charity. It also requires an unusually radical hospitality to let strangers into your church every day of the week.

As we engage in social media, we are displaying our lives in the public sphere. We are creating online personas that are visited, read, shared with others who are online. In this way and many others, our lives are becoming more and more public whether we are aware of it or not. As we post our pictures, our feelings, and our activities online, we become public figures. If you have any doubt about this, go to Google and query your name. A friend of mine did this recently and found seven pages and hundreds of thousands of entries pointing to his name. Taking pictures and videos of people's lives is becoming easier and easier. In fact, these pictures and videos can make news by providing footage of events not covered by the press. Our lives are always on public display, even if we don't intend them to be. And our public opinions matter. Justine Sacco learned this lesson in a most public and embarrassing way. Right before the public relations official boarded an international flight to South Africa, she tweeted an offensive message on Twitter about AIDS. While the plane was in the air, her tweet became viral and sparked worldwide outrage, outrage that eventually cost her her job.[1] A public voice can come with public costs.

And so as we become public people, we need to ask ourselves how we can effectively present our lives so that we can make a positive contribution to the written form of the gospel message through our own blogs, sermons, articles, comments, conversations, and even books. How can this be done in a way that maintains a sense of integrity and the high calling of the gospel?

Public Theology

Theology should be a "critical reflection on the beliefs and practices of the faith community out of which it arises."[2] Theological reflection must not be ignored or neglected but must take precedence in one's life, community, and church. Engaging in theological reflection should be an important task of the individual believer as well as the church's responsibility. The faith community's responsibility is to be engaged in critical reflection that takes seriously the issues of the day precisely because these are matters of life and death. When another African American unarmed boy or man is shot down by a police officer, when another woman is raped, when wars break out and

---

1. See Ashley Southall, "A Twitter Message about AIDS, Followed by a Firing and an Apology," *The New York Times*, December 20, 2013. http://thelede.blogs.nytimes.com/2013/12/20/a-twitter-message-about-aids-africa-and-race/?_php=true&_type=blogs&_r=0.
2. Daniel L. Migliore, *Faith Seeking Understanding* (Grand Rapids: Eerdmans, 2004), xi.

innocent children are killed, theologians are called to try to make sense of these events. Theologians must seek out God and God's face in this broken world so that we can offer some fleeting glimpse of understanding, hope, and peace. Our writings need to encourage the brokenhearted and the downtrodden so that even in their pain, they may see God and recognize God in each other. This makes it crucial for every theologian to engage in public writing. When theology becomes irrelevant, then theology is dead and God's voice is stilled.

Ethicist Stanley Hauerwas noted in a 2011 lecture at Lehigh University that doctors make more moral decisions in a week than most of us may make in a year, and many are life and death decisions. He hinted that most doctors engage far more of these decisions than the average minister. But look at it from the other side. What profession, aside from physicians, works that intensely with what is right and what is wrong than the theologian, the parish priest, the minister, or the reverend? History points to moments when the call to ministry was also a call to public witness. For instance, the civil rights movement of the 1960s gained incredible energy thanks to the leadership of clergy. Speaking from the pulpit, bully or otherwise, has moral force. Be sure of what you say, then use that platform for the sake of the liberating power of the gospel.

And yet we must keep in mind that *all* people are theologians. By following Jesus, one is a theologian.[3] As a theologian, engaging in theological discourse in the public sphere is important. Theology needs to be concerned with how faith interacts with everyday questions and the concerns of society. Theology matters to the people as God matters to those around us and to creation. We are slowly killing the earth. We need to engage in public theology so that we can begin to take steps in reversing the damage we have done to

3. Howard W. Stone and James O. Duke, *How to Think Theologically* (Minneapolis: Augsburg Fortress, 2006), viii.

the earth. Without this public engagement, we continue on the road toward destruction.

Christianity and the Christian faith need to engage in the major issues of society whether they are personal or communal issues. No matter who you are, as a follower of Christ in a world so full of injustice, you have a call to speak good news. And one of the most powerful ways you can do that is by writing publicly in venues previous generations could not access, except through highly censored letters to the editor. Faith has something to say to our most pressing issues, and Christians should engage publicly in these matters.

In February 2012 when a teenage boy named Trayvon Martin was walking home with a bag of Skittles and bottle of iced tea, he was shot by George Zimmerman. This incident sparked national outrage. Demonstrations and rallies took place declaring that racial profiling and racism were deadly evils. During this time, many theologians spoke and wrote about this issue to help us understand the message of a gospel that compels us to love one another despite differences in skin color, ethnicity, culture, and heritage. The killing of yet another African American teenager, Michael Brown, in Ferguson, Missouri, in 2014 consequently created yet more space for prophetic and public writing. And certainly, even as you are reading this essay, you could add a litany of current events that demand a Christian response. This is the power of writing publicly. You too can shape conversations happening not just in your local community but also in the nation and the world. God may be calling you to speak truth in places both near and far.

Theologians are always informed by their circumstances and events shaping the world around them. "A responsible theologian is guided by deliberations on the historic themes of faith, by scripture and tradition, by worship, and by engaged service in the world."[4]

These important aspects need to guide and shape public theological discourse. Theology seeks to understand life. Theology tries to make sense of what we do and the difference between what is wholeness to be relished and what is an illness to be opposed.

When we take seriously the task of theology and engage with the current issues of the day, we will be driven to write publicly. With the rise of pervasive communication technologies and the shrinking of the world because of them, it has become that much more important to write for the public.

Writing Publicly

Many benefits emerge from engaging in public writing. Writing publicly today provides an incredible number of us an opportunity to think critically, engage politically, and write theologically. In contrast, academic writing often focuses on a particular niche of scholarship, a small audience, and a highly technical style of writing. As a result, writing publicly can be a powerful form of theological reflection that just might touch the masses of people online, on social media, and through other online networks that a textbook or heavy academic prose would not necessarily reach.

Writing publicly can be a spiritual exercise as you engage in spiritual yearning as you read, reflect, and write. Writing publicly engages your being, as it means that Christians, non-Christians, religious, and nonreligious people are all coming into a digital space to read and be challenged, moved, and transformed by your writing.

However, many of us have learned to write only academic papers for a classroom setting or perhaps sermons for a Sunday morning service. Writing publicly engages a different set of tools of writing

4. Howard W. Stone and James O. Duke, *How to Think Theologically* (Minneapolis: Augsburg Fortress, 2006), viii.

than academic papers or sermons. It requires you to engage continuously in cultural, world, social, and political scenes so that your theological writing can emerge from such events. To engage in such issues is to engage in the work of social justice, humility, and care for our neighbors. In August 2012, a teenage girl was raped by two boys in a Steubenville, Ohio, high school. Because pictures of the victim and scenes from the violent acts were posted online, this rape case became a national case illustrating violence against women. Theologians wrote publicly about the difficulties that women face due to religion's role in subordinating women. It challenged the way the church views women and the violence that is too often perpetrated against them. In another situation, a law student, Sandra Fluke, made a plea before Congress to have birth control pills covered by health insurance. In response, she was slandered online and called a slut by high-profile radio host Rush Limbaugh. An essay by theologian Susan Thistlethwaite fought back against sexual shaming by paralleling what happened to Fluke with the interpretative traditions of the Bible stories about Mary Magdalene.[5]

It takes a great investment of time and effort to write for a wider audience. Is it worth it? When all things are taken into consideration, writing publicly is necessary and crucial for ministers today, as it may be exactly how God will communicate the good news through you in a rapidly changing world. Our writing must reach people where they are today, which we cannot assume is in our pews or Bible study groups anymore. They are on the Internet. They are tweeting. They are on Facebook. They are writing and reading blogs. To reach out to those who do not enter our churches, we need to adapt our

---

5. Susan Thistlethwaite, "Mary Magdalene to Rush Limbaugh: Your Apology Is Too Little, Too Late," *OnFaith,* March 5, 2012. http://www.faithstreet.com/onfaith/2012/03/05/mary-magdalene-to-rush-limbaugh-your-apology-is-too-little-too-late/10632

forms of outreach and begin to take seriously our task of writing for an audience that does not share our vocabulary, assumptions, or contexts. We must write to convince rather than to chide. We have to remember that God is in the public sphere, not locked up in our churches. God is among the poor, the hungry, the outcast, and the marginalized. Our writing should also be out there where God is. When our writing is specifically out where God is, then it becomes more meaningful, enlightening, and empowering.

For the past three years, writing such reflective pieces has become a natural part of my daily spiritual routine. Writing forces me to understand and engage in our present context, situation, and world. It challenges me to understand God in the midst of pain, agony, joy, and peace. It helps me pay attention to the political, social, cultural, and religious issues of our time and draws me to put into writing some meaningful response that might affect others. Writing publicly has become a necessity for me as much as my daily exercise, eating, and reflecting are. It has become a source of spiritual growth and spiritual nurturing as it nourishes my soul and being.

Through the past three years of writing publicly, I have come to realize the importance of this difficult form of writing. After all, many people today are more influenced by what they read online than what they hear preached on Sunday, let alone what some professor has to say in some dusty book.[6] More and more people find reading online quicker, easier, more accessible, and more enjoyable than listening to sermons. If our people are spending more time reading online, perhaps we too should be more present online so that we can help shape and add to the dynamic theological discourse and theological reflection of God's presence in the world.

---

6. But let us not forget that what professors write and say does influence people who, in turn, will be filling the Internet with blogs five years from now.

Steps to Writing Publicly

To begin to writing publicly you can follow these steps. First, you need to find a place to write publicly. There are many options today where you can begin to write publicly. You can write on a friend's blog site or begin your own blog site. This is a good way to begin the process of writing for the public by writing columns and making posts to other church sites or public websites whose readers may be interested in your writing. It is necessary to find a good site to post, share, and engage in your writing. And remember that your preaching, Facebook posts, and other forms of daily communication are public in some significant sense when you are a ministerial leader, due to the nature of public leadership.

Second, find a relatable and interesting topic to write about. Since an overabundance of material is being posted and shared on the Web, find something that will catch readers' attention. Tie your writing interests to your personal, social, and theological interests. If you as a writer are not interested in a relatable topic of the day, it will be fruitless to engage in that writing process. The topic must be of interest to both the reader and the writer. Thus, you need to keep in touch with the relevant news and issues of the day.

Third, write about issues that people care about. This seems obvious, but it's worth emphasizing. There are many pertinent issues today that need to be addressed theologically and politically. So pick those issues that most directly affect people's lives and are especially important to the community you are called to serve.

Fourth, writing publicly requires that you use everyday language devoid of technical terminology and jargon. This may be difficult to do at the beginning; you might feel that you need to use technical language to sound intelligent and important. However, writing for the public does not require this kind of posture. After all, public writing is for the general public; heavy and technical language in these contexts will only become a hindrance to the reader. In short, readers should not need a dictionary or a thesaurus to read your column. If they do need them, they will not bother reading your work, no matter how insightful.

Fifth, the best public writing often tends to be concise. Attention spans are shorter online.[7] You can count on only so much attention from your readers. Convince them quickly and concisely that your writing matters.

Sixth, treat writing like a habit or a practice. Writing, in some ways, is like exercise. When you exercise regularly, it becomes natural and easy to maintain your routine. However, when you stop the regular pattern of exercise, it becomes harder to get back to it. So many excuses enter the mind, and it becomes almost impossible to fight them back. The same applies to writing. If writing is not a regular part of your daily work, then it will prove difficult if not impossible to be a regular and effective author.

Last, have some fun. Enjoy the benefits of writing beyond your regular audience. Writing publicly can be a life-giving experience. Let's be clear: writing is no easy task. It takes much hard work, but writing should be a flourishing habit and event for both the writer and the reader.

There are many more steps, but just following these six steps can help you begin, continue, and sustain your writing process. In a world yearning for meaning in the midst of so much difficulty, it is especially crucial for you to begin and continue to write publicly.

---

7. There is a great line in the movie *The Big Chill* when Jeff Goldblum, playing the role of a writer for *People*, says in essence, "Everything I write must be short enough to finish in the time readers take in the bathroom" (paraphrased).

Conclusion

We are called to use social media to our advantage to build the church and our communities. We need to be aware of how to swim in these new, roiling waters so that we can make media work in our own faith communities. As a theologian, using media to help share news of hope, justice, peace, and love is important. Chances are, more people out in the media-saturated world are listening to us than people sitting in our pews and classrooms.

In a media-saturated society, media has become our podiums and pulpits. It has become the backdrop and the medium of our messages. More people read media reports than read theological textbooks. More listen to and view media outlets than hear our sermons. That means, of course, that if our message from the pulpit is out of touch with these other sources, our message will not be taken seriously.

The sooner the church catches on to these emerging realities, the better equipped we will be to serve the church and the world, not just in the future but also today. As ecclesial demographics shift all around us, the use of media may now become more than just an attraction to draw in younger members; it may soon become a matter of survival for our communities of faith. The key will be for people like you, leaders with a voice and a perspective, to become known as one of those reliable sources whose information and commentary is thoughtful, accurate, and easy to reach.

In short, we are called today to become *public* theologians who will engage in *public* writing. Our lives, our thoughts, our ideas should make an impact on the world around us. Our gospel understanding and practice should influence the world around us so that together we can all participate in building the reign of God here on earth.

7

Writing Digitally

Adam J. Copeland

Students today write more than ever before, most of it mediated by digital technologies. Take, for example, a typical day in my life. This morning, my wife and I sent five text messages to one another to coordinate drinks with a friend after work. I participated in several conversations with colleagues on Facebook, both in private messages and on public walls where others joined us. I sent four e-mails, one composed on my iPhone while walking down the hall. I typed my credit card number into a crowd-funding website, then shared news of the project on several social media platforms. I checked my digital calendar and added several new appointments. I tweeted a few times with friends at a conference, and now, finally, I have closed my web browser and opened Microsoft Word to work on this chapter. Today, I have written hundreds of words, few of which would be considered formal writing. I haven't touched a pen or paper.

This chapter is meant for the technology savvy and technology averse alike. I do not believe that to succeed in graduate theological education one must join all the hippest social media networks, own the latest iGadget, and commune with computers. While digital awareness is an important component of many vocations today, not all are called to technological innovation. So, if you are worried I am going to suggest that graduate theological education should require you to learn how to write in computer-programming language, you can rest easy (and focus on Greek and Hebrew instead).

Why Digital Writing

My thesis in this chapter is twofold. First, graduate education today requires a certain amount of digital literacy. Becoming digitally literate requires you to pursue questions like, How are God's people communicating today? On what platforms is digital writing occurring? When is technology mediating our lives? Digital literacy does not require you to be cognizant of every text-messaging initialism out there (OMG, no!), but it does warrant a basic understanding of how digital communication technologies affect our life together. Second, beyond achieving basic digital literacy, students pursuing graduate theological education should strive for digital wisdom. The cultivation of such wisdom along with theological, biblical, ecclesial, and pastoral forms of wisdom will help you gain capabilities for translation and communication in digital environments.[1]

Just like the other forms of wisdom pursued in graduate school, digital wisdom does not come all at once. You will gain some digital writing skills in your courses, but you will also need to seek opportunities beyond the classroom. The iterative nature of digital writing makes it challenging for professors to include in specific

---

1. For a book of essays that consider the phrase *digital wisdom*, see Marc Prensky, *From Digital Natives to Digital Wisdom: Hopeful Essays for 21st Century Learning* (Thousand Oaks, CA: Corwin, 2012).

assignments. Many professors do not devote the time or possess the baseline technical skills to learn and then teach the latest digital technologies. Thus, even while more instructors do experiment with assignments and other experiences that emphasize digital writing, it's unwise to rely only on your professors' guidance when it comes to digital literacy and wisdom. Pursuing digital wisdom takes a combination of your own initiative, the collegiality of student peers, and the support of your faculty. No true learning, and no fine writing, is a solo endeavor. Digital writing, especially, calls for a communal approach to study and practice.

What Is Digital Writing?

What do the words *digital writing* actually mean? Not too long ago, students going off to seminary would pack their pens and pencils, newly purchased books, and typewriter. Professors required, after all, that papers be typed—on a typewriter— rather than handwritten. Today, graduate students might arrive on campus with a laptop, Kindle, smartphone, and tablet. Many will take class notes using one or more of these devices. Some professors will ask students to turn in their assignments using the school's content management system, electronic learning platform, or simply by e-mail. Professors will then add electronic comments and grades and return assignments digitally. It's perfectly possible, then, for a traditional essay assignment never to touch actual paper. In some real ways, practically all writing today is digital, and using the word *paper* for *essay* is increasingly anachronistic.

The notion of digital writing is fairly new. Not surprising, our understanding of what constitutes digital writing is still being nuanced, our definitions narrowing and expanding as new technologies arise.[2] For example, JodiAnn Stevenson has described digital writing as "any writing that requires a computer to access it."[3] Others, like Dan Waber, suggest digital writing might be considered writing that, if accessed nondigitally, is diminished.[4] We could also take an inductive approach and describe digital writing with examples such as blogging, texting, online game playing, social networking, e-mailing, and so on. The editors of *Because Digital Writing Matters* define digital writing as "compositions created with, and oftentimes for reading or viewing on, a computer or other device that is connected to the Internet."[5] One may quibble with each of these definitions, but for our purposes they fill in a picture of digital writing that relies on screens, computing devices, and the networks made possible when such devices enable connections between people and ideas.

Another way of understanding the nature of digital writing focuses on the culture in which it takes place. Henry Jenkins, a media scholar, describes us as living in a "participatory culture" today:

> A participatory culture is a culture with relatively low barriers to artistic expression and civic engagement, strong support for creating and sharing one's creations, and some type of informal mentorship whereby what is known by the most experienced is passed along to novices. A participatory culture is also one in which members believe their contributions matter, and feel some degree of social connection with one another (or at least they care what other people think about what they have created).[6]

---

2. See Chris Joseph, "State of the Art," Process, Trace Online Writing Centre, http://tracearchive.ntu.ac.uk/Process/index.cfm?article=131.

3. Ibid.

4. Ibid.

5. National Writing Project, *Because Digital Writing Matters* (San Francisco: Jossey-Bass, 2010), 7.

6. Henry Jenkins, et al., "Confronting the Challenges of Participatory Culture: Media Education for the 21st Century," MacArthur Foundation Reports on Digital and Media Learning (Cambridge, MA: MIT Press, 2009), https://mitpress.mit.edu/sites/default/files/titles/free_download/9780262513623_Confronting_the_Challenges.pdf.

I recently happened upon an illuminating example of this participatory culture. On my personal blog, I posted a short essay concerning local media coverage of national news stories focused on our local community.[7] This is very meta but stay with me! In the post, I suggested a hashtag that captured the sentiments of the post.[8] As is my normal practice, I shared the blog post on Twitter and Facebook. Within twenty-four hours, the original blog post had been shared hundreds of times beyond my personal network. People I did not know discussed the post in their networks—both electronic and otherwise—and expanded the discussion. The hashtag began to be used by many people I had never met and who had not read the original blog post. The day after posting the essay, I received a call from a reporter at the local newspaper who proceeded to interview me. The next day, a story about the blog post, with diverse perspectives from several city leaders, appeared on the front page of the newspaper. My original blog post started with little more than what friends and I often discuss informally, but the participatory culture in which the post appeared aided in its dissemination. In today's society, opinion-based digital writing on a personal blog can drive front-page news.

Elements of Digital Style

The nature of digital writing and the rapid technological changes accompanying it make it difficult to consider in a chapter that will not be updated every few months. Even so, we can take note of

---

7. See Adam J. Copeland, "I'm #AmbivalentAboutFargo and You Should Be Too," *A Wee Blether* (blog), June 9, 2014, http://www.adamjcopeland.com/2014/06/09/im-ambivalentaboutfargo-you-should-be-too/.

8. Using hashtags on some social media sites, such as Twitter and Facebook, is one way to tag content, grouping similar material so that it might be easily found in searches. Hashtags begin with a pound sign, also known as a "hash" (e.g., #MNTwins or #Obama).

several themes related to digital writing that have developed in the past decade or so.

First, the norms of digital writing change quickly, so we must consistently develop new skills and remain aware. New words can become commonplace in a short time. For example, the notion of *going viral*—as in massive sharing of a YouTube video, digital picture, or online campaign—made its way into dictionaries only in the mid-2000s. The ebb and flow of digital trends can make them difficult to navigate. One month, taking a selfie (a self-portrait using a smartphone) and posting it on social networks with a certain phrase can be the new, hip practice. Just a few months later, such a practice might be perceived as old hat, perhaps even uncool.

We can see this shift in the development of Facebook, for instance. When Facebook began, it was open only to students at elite colleges. When it was available to them, high school students flocked to the network. For a time, Facebook was *the place* for online social interaction. However, as Facebook's user base expanded, its popularity among youth has declined. Today, most of America's youth have Facebook accounts, but they choose to spend much of their time on other social networks.

The shifting context in which digital writing occurs today makes it an exciting, ever-changing practice. It is understandable that amid the demands of graduate school, keeping up with the latest digital trends may not be your top priority. Even so, taking note of digital changes—once they have become somewhat commonplace—will serve you well.

Such changing norms can have significant consequences beyond the digital realm. For example, the font Comic Sans became popular in the late 1990s and was used in advertisements, in e-mails, and on hundreds of church bulletin boards. In the early 2000s, however, a backlash developed, including several campaigns to ban Comic Sans, especially the use of the font on material regarding serious subject matter. Thus, applying for a job today with Comic Sans on your résumé might help you to stick out from the competition, but only negatively. Successfully navigating today's cultural context requires keeping up to date on ever-changing digital norms.

Second, due to its visual nature, digital writing emphasizes *design*.[9] Document design includes your decisions concerning, for example, how much white space to leave on the page, font selection, proximity and alignment of design elements, use of pictures, citation of sources, and other, often visual choices. Smart document design ensures that the material you turn in reflects the best of the genre, whether a formal term paper or a web-forum post. A few examples: most web-based writing platforms allow for hyperlinks rather than long web addresses, bullets rather than dashes; if an image supports your argument, include it artfully; in e-mails (often read quickly on devices with small screens) include ample paragraph breaks and bolding when appropriate. Approaching document-design decisions as important aspects of your digital writing will help your work look professional, reflect its correct genre, and show creativity.

Third, when I was in seminary the phrase, "Well . . . it depends on the context" was used so often it became sort of a campus-wide joke. We discussed context often because context matters—in biblical texts, in teaching and preaching, and certainly in faith-related conversations. Context matters in digital writing too, and many new media platforms bring fresh challenges for negotiating context.

My friends who are elementary school teachers share entertaining stories of running into their students outside of school. Often, the students don't know what to make of the fact that their teacher can

---

9. For an argument calling for faculty to appreciate design decisions in their assignments, see Evan Snider, "Teaching Document Design, Not Formatting Requirements," *ProfHacker* (blog), *Chronicle of Higher Education*, Dec 10, 2010, http://chronicle.com/blogs/profhacker/teaching-document-design-not-formatting-requirements/29041.

exist outside the school building. One friend reports a first grader was aghast at seeing her in the grocery store. "What are *you* doing here?" she asked. "Buying dinner" was apparently not an acceptable answer. Such an experience is an example of context collapse. As social media scholar danah boyd explains, "A context collapse occurs when people are forced to grapple simultaneously with otherwise unrelated social contexts that are rooted in different norms and seemingly demand different social responses."[10] With the rise of social networks, context collapse can occur while you sit in the comfort of your own home.

It can be both thrilling and terrifying when contexts collapse. Comment feeds can be places of particular challenge. I know more than one pastor with a story of posting a picture on Facebook that stirred trouble with certain congregation members. You will need to make your own decisions about how to manage the different contexts of your life in graduate school. Will you seek to connect with professors on social networks? Aware of future job interviews, will you censor political or sensitive personal posts in some manner? How will you balance in-person conversation and technology-mediated interactions?[11] And, most important of all, will you spare your high school friends from dozens of theology-related updates?

A main reason context collapse occurs so easily is the nonlinear nature of digital writing. We generally read printed books from beginning to end. Their printed form enables the function of reading left to right, from page one to the last. We often encounter digital writing, however, without much context. A reader might find a blog post addressing an ongoing concern or responding to a series

---

10. danah boyd, *It's Complicated: The Social Lives of Networked Teens* (New Haven: Yale University Press, 2014) 31.
11. See Adam J. Copeland, "Pastors Double Down on Facebook: The Boundary-Setting, Dual Identity of Pastors with Two Facebook Accounts," in *Media, Religion, History, Culture: Selected Essays from the 4th Elon University Media and Religion Conference*, ed. Anthony Hatcher (Bloomington, IN: AuthorHouse, 2014).

of other posts without any notion of the larger conversation. In a similar way, some tweets, comment feeds, or Facebook posts might seem problematic without an understanding of what came before. The nature of digital writing makes awareness of context—always an important concern in theological education—even more vital.

Liking, Retweeting, and Pinning: Platforms for Writing Digitally

I have suggested that most of our writing today can be considered digital writing, in part, to guard against narrowing our understanding of digital writing to social networks alone. Even so, I would be remiss not to consider some new media spaces where digital writing is occurring today.

Facebook

As of this writing, Facebook remains the most populated social network in the world. However, it is important to note that Facebook use has shifted in recent years, and other social networks have more cache among certain demographic groups. Writing digitally on Facebook depends on the functionality selected. Sharing articles, liking posts, and commenting on news items occurs in the main news feed section of the site. More private writing can occur with the messages section of the site where you can narrow your audience. Facebook is built on a network of "friends," suggesting a certain amount of familiarity with your audience for any writing on the site. Unlike other networks, there is practically no character limit to what you might post.

Twitter

The 140-character limit of Twitter makes it a network for creative, crafted, concise communication. Twitter sets itself apart from some social networks by allowing users to follow, and be followed by, people and organizations with whom they have had no previous contact. Many Twitter users rarely post themselves and mainly use the network as a platform to gather opinions, news, and information. Searching a hashtag (for example, #ELCA) on Twitter brings up recent tweets tagged by users as relating to the category or theme of the hashtag.

Image Sharing

Sites like Pinterest, Instagram, and Snapchat have gained in popularity in recent years, suggesting an interest in image-rich digital material. Even Vine, a platform for creating and sharing seven-second videos, might be understood as related to this visual messaging orientation. Facebook algorithms now highlight status updates with pictures over text-only updates. If the rise of images on social networks corresponds to a true preference for visual communication, you may do well to consider how visual rhetoric might be employed in your theological education. For instance, how might theological concepts be represented with infographics? Is there value today in representing biblical texts with visual media?

Text Messaging

One value of text messaging is its affordance of *asynchronous* communication. While phone calls require listeners to speak to one another at the same time (synchronously), text messaging allows for extended conversations to take place without needing to speak *right now* with your conversation partner. Like Twitter, text messages work best when concise, but their writing should not be considered inconsequential. Texting is a powerful medium for digital writing. Consider the ubiquity of text messaging as you pursue graduate theological education. I took my pastoral care courses before texting was common, but when I served as a pastor, I certainly had to work out how I would respond to parishioners' text messages at all times of the day or night. During seminary, texting can be a valuable medium for supporting your classmates through the rigors of study or razzing them when your favorite sports team beats theirs. In short, well-timed, thoughtful text messages can connect us in powerful ways. Artful language use is as important when typed with your thumbs as when written by hand.

Blogs

I must confess a certain personal affinity for blogging: I started a blog midway through my time as a seminary student and kept writing consistently for more than seven years. I find blogging helpful for building writing skills, processing new information, sharing ideas, and receiving feedback in short order. For a piece to go from submitted to published in traditional academic publishing can take years. On my blog, I can post something in minutes—and it's not the end of the world if it includes a typo. The same intellectual curiosity that makes for success in graduate school is easily lived-out online. Many students become fairly prolific bloggers. Even as I confess my affinity, however, I do not expect blogging to be the best digital writing medium for everyone. Indeed, I require blogging assignments in my classes and receive mixed responses from students. Like all digital media platforms, however, it may be worthwhile to attempt to blog for a time and judge your results from actual experience. Even if you do not become a regular blogger, understanding the basics of blogging platforms (WordPress, Blogger, Tumblr) is important knowledge in today's information society.

Building Skills in Participatory Culture

As mentioned above, Henry Jenkins's notion of participatory culture describes our social context today as one that values and enables digital creation, sharing, connecting, and networking. Along with core literacies of reading and writing, Jenkins argues we should teach new media skills in primary and secondary education. Cultural competency requires an understanding of new media, and Jenkins suggests several core media-literacy skills. Below, I highlight four of these skills as I consider how they apply to graduate theological education.[12]

Appropriation

Appropriation has to do with taking an existing piece of culture and modifying it for some other event, purpose, or audience. Of course, appropriation is not a new phenomenon—it's found throughout the Bible for instance—but digital technologies allow for easier sharing and modifying. If you stay open to the possibilities, you will find ample opportunities for appropriation in graduate school. Two examples follow. First, Pastor John Vest shares an example from a youth group's retelling of the road to Emmaus passage (Luke 24:13-35) by way of an imaginary Twitter conversation:

> Characters: @cleodisc is Cleopas, @guy is the unnamed character, @j-hizzle is Jesus.
>
> @cleodisc: omg, weird bearded guy just joined me and @guy on the road to emmaus #awkward
>
> @guy: weird bearded guy doesn't know about @j-hizzle
>
> @j-hizzle: these guys are fools

12. Jenkins et al., "Confronting the Challenges," 19ff.

@cleodisc: I just spent 10 minutes talking about @j-hizzle to weird bearded guy

@guy: weird bearded guy has strange scars on his hands

@j-hizzle: just taught these fools the word #inception

@cleodisc: invited weird bearded guy to break bread

@cleodisc: dude, weird bearded guy is @j-hizzle! #embarrassed[13]

The Twitter conversation retells the text in a way that appreciates digital communication and sheds new light on the passage.

Second, when working with a church considering leaving my denomination, I came across a document that addressed some of the church's concerns. Because it was authored by legal staff in our church headquarters, the document read very formally, and the members of the committee did not think it would communicate clearly to the congregation. So, in the spirit of appropriation, we rewrote the two-page document, giving it an informal, kitchen-table-conversation tone (while clearly citing the original document). We shared the appropriated piece with the congregation and posted it on my blog.[14] The post received over three hundred fifty Facebook likes and shares. In comparison, the formal document on the denominational website has received eighty-one likes. Digital technologies allow for exciting new ways of connecting, remaking, and distributing ideas.

13. John Vest, "#RoadtoEmmaus," Adventures in Post-Christendom, July 7, 2011, JohnVest.com, http://johnvest.com/2011/07/28/roadtoemmaus/.
14. Adam J. Copeland, "Is the PCUSA Going Down the Tubes?," A Wee Blether (blog), Sept. 5, 2013, http://www.adamjcopeland.com/2013/09/05/is-the-pcusa-going-down-the-tubes/.

Multitasking

Have you been reading this chapter with your full attention? Have you glanced at your phone or read an e-mail or sent a tweet—or done all three—in the last fifteen minutes? Appreciation for multitasking has risen along with the increases in digital writing and technologies. Multitasking is a two-edged sword. On the one hand, it allows you to take in the full complement of your experiences without getting too focused on one event. Thank goodness, for instance, that parents can hear their children crying while they cook dinner. On the other hand, depth of attention is important in seminary. As Jenkins suggests, part of educational success today includes learning "when and how to pay close attention to a specific input as well as when and how to scan the environment searching for meaningful data."[15] Scanning your environment and becoming aware of the variety of the opportunities around you is an important new media literacy skill; deciding when to focus your full attention on one experience is a mark of digital wisdom.

As you learn to become successful in seminary, you may need to try several approaches to moving from multitasking to focusing your attention on one experience. Some writers prefer to write in silence while others enjoy soft music in the background. I know one author who selects one song for each writing project and plays that song on repeat until the project is completed. I will often turn off my e-mail program while I write a longer piece. I have a friend who sets an alarm on his phone for every hour while he is writing. When the alarm goes off, he scrolls through Twitter for seven minutes before going back to writing for another hour. Because of the need for online research, digital writing may pose problems particularly for the easily distracted. Such challenges will not go away upon

---

15. Jenkins et al., "Confronting the Challenges," 36.

graduation, so finding how you write and learn best is worth committed experimentation. Ultimately, appreciating when to multitask, and finding wisdom to know when a task calls for undivided attention, will serve you well in graduate school and life beyond.

Collective Intelligence

In digital culture, the notion of individual achievement is often overshadowed by collective intelligence. Digital tools lower barriers of communication, support learning from others you have never met, and simplify the pooling of resources. It's common to see a young theologian post an evocative thesis on Facebook or a pastor ask for advice in an online forum. Even within the humanities, a field historically focused on single-author books and papers, scholars are claiming a new "digital humanities" approach that emphasizes digital tools, group achievement, cross-disciplinary conversation, and public sharing of ongoing research. Such moves should be welcomed in the church and by theologically minded graduate students, for we have long appreciated that no one person has a corner on the truth.

You can support such a philosophy by sharing resources and ideas freely. Of course, it's important to attribute authorship when possible, but digital tools like wikis, forums, even e-mail help us connect and share information in ways unimaginable just a few years ago. Consider posting your term papers online. Form study groups and share resources with others. Upload digital versions of class notes. Tweet the best quotes from your classes. In short, share widely so that we can learn together.

Play

It may seem strange to consider play and graduate school together, but digital tools break down a strict dichotomy between learning and play. Teachers are increasingly considering the educational possibilities of gaming, participating in immersive digital environments, and other means of playful engagement. For example, digital tools may support the memorization required for learning a new language. Play can allow for the construction of new possibilities, imagining novel events, and appreciating other perspectives. Digital writing, in particular, can proceed playfully as information and communication technologies allow for fast-paced wit and banter.

Digital Wisdom

Like all forms of wisdom, digital wisdom develops slowly. To have any hope of becoming digitally wise, you must form a firm foundation of digital literacy. You need not participate in every digital tool available, but you would be well served to gain digital awareness, to watch how digital writing and culture changes over time, and to consider connections to the gospel. Since in graduate theological education today it's impossible to avoid writing digitally, consider its ways and be wise.

8

Writing Purposefully

Melinda A. McGarrah Sharp

Writing purposefully is sacred communication that engages human experiences, addresses communities across time, and dares to bring voice to the mysteries of divine presence. Writing purposefully articulates theological claims even while discerning and perhaps challenging them. It is your responsibility and yours alone to write with purpose about your most deeply held convictions. However, this does not mean you are alone.[1]

Seminaries host communities of writers in conversation. Diverse theological commitments that may or may not align with yours coexist within and across seminaries. It is therefore easy to slip into dehumanizing speech that opposes positions and people in uncharitable ways. Dehumanization—deliberate or unintentional—is a strategic process of defining *human being* as an exclusive category in which not every person belongs. This chapter will help you avoid

---

1. I am grateful for insightful conversations on the subject of this chapter with M. Perkins, K. McClean, my students, and volume editors.

unintentional dehumanization in your writing and instead write purposefully as an intentional practice, commitment, and process of Christian ministries.

Practice: Cultivating Habits of Sacred Communication

The practice of writing purposefully includes attending to both your habits and your contexts. Writing purposefully is a disciplined practice of thoughtful habits before, during, and after each writing task. Some seminary writing tasks can seem mundane and others exceedingly intimidating. Engaging the mundane with purpose and the intimidating with both humility and confidence will help you write well.

Beyond writing mechanics, writing theologically is a disciplined practice of sacred communication with an inherent moral demand to write responsibly. While writing can seem isolating or individualistic, it is and should be communal at its heart. Theologically significant writing dares to represent human and divine in ways that serve pastoral functions, exceed any one audience, and bridge experiential worlds. Abrahamic faiths share the conviction originating in the Hebrew Scriptures that human beings—all human beings—are made in the image and likeness of God. This conviction is called the *imago Dei*, or image of God.

Respect for people is thus not optional for us but indeed fuels love of God and neighbor. *Imago Dei* suggests that as God's creation made in God's image and likeness, I, you, and all people participate in the life of God in our shared human creaturely form. Writing is a crucial part of how this basic sacred and moral conviction becomes embodied differently across theological positions within Christianity and even across religious traditions. The human activity of writing fosters a deep practice of divine participation. Sacred mysteries that form the basis of communal belonging are revealed in texts and wrestled with in texts. Oral histories and sung traditions draw communities together into sacred storytelling, itself a kind of living text.[2]

Believe it or not, your writing contributes to sacred communication. What writing habits do you have that remind you that your writing is sacred? What writing habits do you need to let go of because they impede your appreciation for the sacred nature of writing? The theological claim of *imago Dei* requires that the divine in me greet the divine in you, because we human beings are created to participate in divinity.[3] The deepest, most trusting, and healthiest relationships are places where love of self, other human beings, God, and all creation converge. Words form and inform these relationships in and across living contexts. From e-mails to term papers, your writing matters. Your writing is a sacred matter.

Practice: Writing Where You Live

You begin any writing task in the middle of your context—the stories and textures that form you. Even when stretching to write about topics that seem far removed from your life experiences, you write where you live. This requires habits of self-reflection in which you make time to put words to the vital experiences, places, institutions, and people who shape you and whom you shape. By writing purposefully, you also always engage deep histories of powerful words. This requires your critical engagement around power as it relates to the histories of words and ideas. As such, your writing is never constrained to one small audience but indeed exceeds its own

---

2. Luke A. Powery, *Dem Dry Bones: Preaching, Death, and Hope* (Minneapolis: Fortress Press, 2012).
3. This idea permeates the work of Archbishop Desmond Tutu as evidenced in his many books, speeches, and sermons.

necessarily limited context while also being rooted in it. Seminary will ask you to connect this historical and intercultural context of writing to your contemporary context today.

In fact, you might write today for a particular audience, but you never know what new audiences you might gather in the future. So also, sacred texts written long ago become accessible again in every generation. While cultivating habits of purposeful writing within your current seminary, faith community, and immediate circles of influence is important, your writing is rarely limited to these discrete audiences. Consider the context of everything you write, identifying intended audiences while clarifying longer-term implications.[4]

Your theological writing contributes to three intertwined conversations: an academic context, a faith community context, and a public context.[5] First, in your formal seminary term papers you share in academic conversations that have been going on long before you and will continue long after you. This requires knowing the academic contexts and conversations that surround any one writing topic or task. A student of mine once said that she prefers to leave the academic study to the academic experts and be freed to do ministry. Yet, the academy is made up of human beings who need to hear your unique perspective as much as anyone else's perspective. Be careful not to think your contribution to academic conversations is unimportant, especially when that dialogue feels most intimidating. It can seem that academic conversation removed from immersion in daily life is all that matters to the academy, but this is far from the case.

Second, your academic writing contributes to ecclesial conversations. Your theological writing comments both explicitly

4. Mary Clark Moschella, *Ethnography as a Pastoral Practice: An Introduction* (Cleveland: Pilgrim, 2008).
5. David Tracy, *The Analogical Imagination: Christian Theology and the Culture of Pluralism* (New York: Crossroad, 1981).

and implicitly on religious practices and therefore contributes to conversations about what is church and what is religion, both categories under deep debate today.[6] Your writing will be instrumental for how you write yourself into the life of faith. Where will you uphold traditional theological commitments? Where will your work breathe new life into dysfunctional institutional structures? What forms of community will come together to create new wineskins? Your writing will reveal to you and to your faith community your strategies for both investing in and divesting of ecclesial structures.

Third, your theological writing is part of your public voice. All theologians are public theologians; the fact that you attend seminary and soon will have the academic credentials of seminary training behind your name places you in a public role. You may have already begun receiving questions tied to this role of public academic. You may have noticed some relationships shifting now that you are contemplating or investing in formal theological education. You will be responsible to speak from an informed position on a multitude of issues both predictable and unanticipated. Seminary is the best place to cultivate and practice your public voice in that you will be surrounded by resources and people to support, challenge, and empower you.

Academic, ecclesial, and public conversations are important and call forth the purposeful cultivation of your public voice. If and when you are tempted to think, "Why does this assignment [or paper, class, reading, study time, editing] matter to my ministry?," remember that your writing is a rich opportunity for you to articulate connections and disconnections between your academic writing and your ministerial practices.

6. For one of many discussions of this change, see Diana Butler Bass, *Christianity after Religion: The End of Church and the Birth of a New Spiritual Awakening* (New York: HarperOne, 2013).

Your purposeful writing practices make a difference because they communicate and embody theological convictions about what it means to be a human being here and now.[7] How you write about yourself, other people, and creation is intricately related to the activity of loving and being in relationship with God. Your purposeful writing in seminary will help you begin to articulate these inherently sacred and moral relationships. You will have opportunities to address some of these dynamics in your theological writing; this matters both within and across diverse contexts.

Commitments: Composition, Critical Engagement, Conversation

Seminary writing asks you to write about religion and faith in the world, connecting your personal commitments to local and global contexts. This will stretch you! How will you write purposefully when deep divisions and intense contrasting opinions surround your topic? Respectful writing is more important today than ever—especially engaging the often taboo topics of religion and politics with simultaneous if sometimes invisible intersections with race, gender, sexuality, nationality, age, ability, socioeconomic location, neighborhood, and other markers of identity.

As public conversations become increasingly divisive, writers should be concerned not only as global citizens but also as theologians, ministers, and faithful people. Paying attention to purposeful writing is more than a matter of so-called political correctness. *Imago Dei* posits that all human beings are created in the image and likeness of God. While steadfastly mysterious, one moral

---

7. The way that any one theological denomination or doctrine or system of belief works out this claim is called that theology's theological anthropology, or a theology's understanding of human beings. For example, see M. Shawn Copeland, *Enfleshing Freedom: Body, Race, and Being* (Minneapolis: Fortress Press, 2009).

imperative is clear: all human beings share in the divine life, and the divine life shares in all human creatures.

Writing purposefully therefore involves a commitment to uphold human dignity. This is easier said than done as humans have a propensity to misunderstand and indeed misrepresent each other, despite our best intentions. Writing always risks misrepresenting. In fact, misunderstanding each other often forms the context of the occasional and miraculous moments of deep mutual understanding shared in human relationships, particularly where diverse faith and cultural practices converge.[8] The difficult process of staying in relationship while discovering our misunderstandings can lead to a deeper, more mutual understanding. It is crucial then to aim for clarity in writing, knowing that clarity will emerge more sharply for you amid the risks of crafting words, editing your writing, and placing your writing in relationship with readers. What might a substantial commitment to uphold human dignity look like when you type term papers, craft sermons, or compose Twitter updates on mobile devices?

Writing purposefully beckons at least three commitments. First, commit to exercising your personal creativity in writing composition. Pay close attention to your language choices word by word. Strive to compose the best, most faithful words each moment allows. As you compose, you will rely on familiar ways of describing the world even as you reach for new ways to speak about mysteries, uncertainties, joys, and terrors. After all, religion concerns suffering and end-times just as it concerns birth and beauty.

You write into this multiplicity and tension, carving the contours of your voice with your writing. Author Anne Lamott charges writers to take on this audacious task little by little, word by word.[9]

---

8. Melinda A. McGarrah Sharp, *Misunderstanding Stories: Toward a Postcolonial Pastoral Theology* (Eugene, OR: Pickwick, 2013).

You will be tempted to stop at the end of your first draft, before the conclusion, when you run out of time, when you have exhausted your reach for words, and when your writing struggles for a place in the midst of competing and equally important commitments. However, writing purposefully exercises your commitments beyond this first movement.

Second, commit to editing your work, rereading it with a critical eye. As you compose words, you also narrate the shape of your life's vocation.[10] Take time to behold your work. Why does it seem natural to describe the world in *this way* and not *that way* to you? What new is emerging that challenges familiar word choices and sentence patterns? What habits have you developed to speak about people and places different from you? For me, a theoretical move from modernity to postmodernity, from simplicities to complexities, and from singularities to multiplicities provokes me to compose fewer singular words and more plural words. I am shaped by the Enlightenment, which strives for *the* single correct answer, and I catch much of this in editing.[11] Notice the incredible insights, such as multiplicity, that might emerge in your editing.

As you edit your informal and formal writing, learn to recognize your patterns and preferences by rereading writing from previous semesters or times in your life. Prolific writer Stephen King claims that the first draft is writing to yourself, while editing allows you to write for others.[12] Editing is not only difficult because of the time it requires; editing is also difficult because it requires writers to probe our hard work at the level of each word to reveal, clarify, and

---

9. Anne Lamott, *Bird by Bird: Some Instructions on Writing and Life* (New York: Anchor, 1995).
10. Mary Catherine Bateson, *Composing a Life* (New York: Grove, 1989).
11. For example, I would edit "the history of pastoral care" to "one way to understand practices of pastoral care historically" to signal suspicions that postmodernism brings to Enlightenment hopes for grasping singular truth claims.
12. Stephen King, *On Writing: A Memoir of the Craft*, 10th anniv. ed. (New York: Scribner, 2010).

even challenge underlying commitments. Yet embracing the editing process is essential for purposeful writing and spiritual growth.

Third, commit to write in relationship with readers. The practice of forming words affects communal life. We human beings exercise our deepest commitments face to face.[13] My words are tested not only in laborious acts of private writing but also when my *I* shares words with a *you* and genuinely seeks a response. As distances between human beings grow over historical, contextual, embodied, and virtual spaces, we can forget that readers are real people, and my *I* can lose the heightened sense of responsibility and social decorum to treat a *you* well in my writing.

Let us not be deceived into believing that distance between writer and reader is novel. Writing is itself always systematically removed from experience by reflective pauses required to compose and edit. As more voices are more accessible, it is easier and perhaps more overwhelming to regard a reading audience generously and respectfully across various distances.[14] In addition to writing commitments of composition and editing, writing purposefully is a commitment to regard readers as full human beings. Cultivate a robust imagination as you consider the readers who may receive and respond to your writing.

Commitment: What's at Stake?

Writing purposefully holds together these three commitments, composition, critical engagement through editing, and conversation, as a process. Seminary writing informs a lifetime commitment to

13. This idea is developed by influential thinkers from Martin Buber to Emmanuel Levinas.
14. See, for example, Miguel De La Torre and Stacey M. Floyd-Thomas, eds., *Beyond the Pale: Reading Ethics from the Margins* (Louisville, KY: Westminster John Knox, 2011), or the classic essay, Robert Allen Warrior, "Canaanites, Cowboys, and Warriors," *Christianity and Crisis* 49 (1989–1990), 261–65.

purposeful writing. Writing reveals who you understand yourself to be as well as the kind of world in which you live. In this way, language is a deeply political tool and template. Your language can be used to connect and to distance, to mend and to destroy. What kind of world are you writing toward? What are you writing against? What supports you? How do you relate to other people and places? What arcs and tensions structure your unfolding stories? Which larger stories do you shape and which shape you?

All writing, from an e-mail to a semester-long project, needs to answer the essential question, What's at stake? Why is *this community event* or *that theological argument* important? Historically, violence between groups works through processes of strategic dehumanization in language often based on seemingly tangible identity markers. Simply stated, some people become important at the expense of other people. Dehumanizing writing is writing that either subtly or blatantly attacks the fundamental dignity that all human beings share with God by being created in God's image. Writing that harms even one person or excludes anyone from the category of person affects the humanity we all share. Writing purposefully is a commitment to be careful with each and every word, because you know what is at stake.

Purposeful writing carries an agenda to depict human beings as human through images, examples, pronouns, and especially when disagreeing with someone else. For this reason, though grammatically correct, writers must be especially careful with the pronouns *us* and *them*, *we* and *they*, *those* and *these*. Christian Scriptures reveal the seriousness that undergirds dualistic existential sorting: wheat and chaff, lambs and goats, harvest and weeds. Indeed, these textual categories tempt writers to sort humans into doom or glory. In theological writing, pronouns take on metaphorical weight with grave consequences. Historical violence takes the pattern of convincing a people that their flourishing depends on the destruction of another.[15] Writing can support and resist this kind of oppression (sometimes simultaneously!). And so writing is rarely morally neutral. How do you depict human beings through your images, examples, pronouns, references, inclusions, and exclusions?

Purposeful writing attends to representation. What does a *we* in your writing represent and imply about a *them*? The strategy of defining "some people" out of the category of person is an oppressive force at work in the politics of representation. This doesn't just happen but evolves slowly and slyly over time. To resist this urge in your writing, consider where you find your authority as a writer. Whom are you authorized to speak for and to speak about in your writing? Who do you imagine is and is not in your intended audience?

Clarity about your authority in relation to your audiences is a matter of theological discernment, which you can and should address in and through your writing. Your habits of composing words, editing, and cultivating a robust and gracious imaginative engagement with reader relationships will help you meet the challenges of writing purposefully. Your ongoing studies of sacred texts, religious histories, and patterns and practices of human interaction in relation to faith communities will convince you that writing is power.

Your writing is powerful; use it purposively.

---

15. See Beverly E. Mitchell, *Plantations and Death Camps: Religion, Ideology and Human Dignity* (Minneapolis: Fortress Press, 2009); and Christena Cleveland, *Disunity in Christ: Uncovering the Hidden Forces That Keep Us Apart* (Downers Grove, IL: InterVarsity, 2013). See also Frantz Fanon, *Black Skin, White Masks*, trans. Charles L. Markmann (New York: Grove Press, 1967).

A Powerful Process

Spiraling around your seminary education, personal history, and unfolding vocation is a writing process with both relational and transformative power. One tweet or a paragraph in a longer piece carries enormous power with potentially enduring consequences. Technology makes it even more tempting to treat lightly your easy access to writing.

However, acknowledging the power your writing can wield can also infuse you with writer's block. Each act in which you dare to write purposefully will affect how you see what you have written before and what you will write into the future. Writing can seem linear when moving one piece of writing from composition into editing and then out into the world, or at least into your professor's inbox. Yet, no piece of writing exists in isolation. Writing is a cyclical process.

Purposeful writing incorporates personal, communal, and historical understanding. In time, this process reveals moments of exceptional clarity but is never quite finished. First, write to understand your own experiences. From your seminary application's statement of purpose to your ordination papers, writing for self-understanding beckons the power of an attuned ear. Personal writing practices such as journaling offer important spiritual supports to help prevent burnout; to clarify and name ideas; to remember and learn from experiences; to form, reform, and celebrate goals; and to live a full and meaningful life. Internships, year in ministry programs, supervised ministry, apprenticeships, clinical pastoral education (CPE) experiences, and immersion courses all offer rich opportunities for cultivating self-understanding through writing. Writing for the purpose of deepening self-awareness requires that you become vulnerable to learning from your own experiences.

Second, write to connect with other people. Even as you work to understand your own experiences, writing purposefully has the power to bridge experiential worlds. The bridges we create and sustain exceed either one of us. The first time in my personal history that two dear friends ended a relationship I remember realizing that I needed to shift my relationship with each partner even while grieving the loss of the pair. In art, two parallel red lines on a white page equal three—each red line and the newly created white line of negative space between them.[16] Writing contributes to the shape of relationships. When you write, consider how you treat others by your implied invitations and exclusions. Purposeful writing dares to assume potential connections that exceed any one author.

Third, write to understand historical arcs. Your writing has the potential to connect with histories that can seem quite distant in time and space. You will read histories of sacred texts, of heartbreaking and exciting strategies of international development undertaken by religious communities over time, of complex roles of religion in historical conflicts, and of ways in which faith weaves in and through both oppression and liberation, both suffering and hope. Historical certainties you learned were foregone will open with fresh and painful possibilities. Mysterious sacred texts and faith practices will be set in very human and many times violent historical contexts. Allow yourself to learn and challenge how you think histories matter today.

The power of purposeful writing weaves a vocation within larger contexts of faith and life that far exceed any one human being but with implications for all human beings. Put words to your own experiences, words you have carried for a long time woven with new words of challenge and hope. Write purposefully.

---

16. Austin Kleon, *Steal Like an Artist: 10 Things Nobody Told You about Creativity* (New York: Workman, 2012).

Ten Strategies for Writing Purposefully

1. Pre-edit. Why are you writing? Is it to fulfill an assignment, respond to an invitation, make sermon notes, journal, e-mail? Demonstrate your faithful response to this *why*. Ask questions about expectations. Make a schedule of drafts working backward from the due date. Covenant with a writing partner to stay on schedule.

2. Rewrite everything. No writer—even a professional writer or a graduating student writing the last paper of the last class of the last semester—can produce a final draft on the first try. We can all easily slip into dehumanizing speech without recognizing it, because much dehumanizing speech is both grammatically correct and a cultural and historical habit. Commit to read, edit, rewrite, and reread everything you write.

3. Clarify voice and pronouns. Traditionally, formal academic writing is written in the third person, distancing the writer's voice from the writing. However, all disciplines bear the burden of accounting for authorial standpoint. Academic writing depends on a self-aware and self-reflective author. When you use first person, clarify and clearly define your use of *we*. On what authority are you speaking for a particular *we*?

4. Be self-reflexive. Use the first person pronoun *I* to speak about your own experiences whenever possible. Self-reflexivity is a posture of intentional self-reflection. First person carries the assumption and moral demand to allow anyone to speak for himself or herself, no matter how shaky or inexperienced in speaking out. Guard against writing about yourself, or anyone else, as if you do or could exist in isolation. Rather, consider the consequences of your words within a dynamic world of interconnectivity.

5. Refer to people as people. Other people are also people; therefore, refer to other people as people. Words like *neighbor, person, brother or sister* or *people who are made poor* are more respectful and less dehumanizing than terms like *these people* or *those people* or *the poor.* Foreground common humanity.

6. Follow style guides and use inclusive language. Follow seminary style guides that outline expectations for both formal academic work and online and on-campus speech. Use proper citations. Exceed minimal expectations. Use inclusive language. It is no longer acceptable to use masculine language (for example, mankind) to refer to all humans. Gender-specific pronouns are widening thanks to critical theory. Check your writing for tendencies to exclude based on identity markers such as gender, race, class, nationality, and more. Be specific about your identity-based claims.

7. Unpack and unmask your epistemology.[17] As you gain proficiency with theological terms and concepts, remember that your role as public theologian includes translation between forms of discourse. Don't pack too much into one sentence or paragraph. Always unpack your epistemology or how you know what you claim to know. What sources inform your claims? One way writers bury their epistemologies is to mask them as self-evident truths that any reasonable and faithful person would know. Try to unpack technical terms. Read drafts aloud to a friend outside seminary to notice where you need to clarify what you mean.

8. Delete or define *the.* The word *the* can unnecessarily creep into your writing. When you mean to be singular and certain,

---

17. "Unmask your epistemology" is a phrase that needs unpacking. I know what I mean, but I need to explain it because both *unmask* and *epistemology* have particular meanings within theological and postcolonial discourses.

use *the*. Delete *the* when you lack authority to speak on behalf of an entity or to avoid confusing complex concepts for self-evident truths. Common misuses of *the* include "the church," "the homeless," "the world," as if any of these are singular or could be defined and described with universal consensus by only one voice.

9. Resist dualisms. Dualisms are deeply embedded in language: good or bad, up or down, in or out, soul or body, right or wrong. Resist these dualistic frameworks. Simple dualisms always oversimplify life experiences. Human beings negotiate life in a dynamic middle rather than at one of two opposing extremes set in stone. Writing against dualisms will draw you into creativity.

10. Collaborate and celebrate. While writing can feel lonely, it can and should be a communal endeavor. Develop networks of writers and readers to support your writing in and beyond seminary. Celebrate every act of writing completed. Offer to celebrate when your colleagues complete writing. Share in humanity's creative abundance by avoiding unintentional dehumanization in your writing. In so doing, you will celebrate the art of writing purposefully.

9

Writing Personally

Raj Nadella

I remember spending long hours in the library working on my first seminary paper about Christology in the Gospel of Matthew. I was certainly driven by a desire to produce a well-researched and clearly articulated paper, but I had a more important goal in mind while writing the paper. I was far more interested in producing the kind of paper my instructor would consider excellent. I was obviously interested in securing a good grade. Beyond that, however, as far as I was concerned, I was not just writing the paper for that instructor's class. I was writing it *for* him. Like most forms of writing, papers written as part of class requirements are often written for others and with others in mind. In my case, part of this notion of writing the paper for the instructor stemmed from a keen awareness of receiving education in a context where the teacher was the center of teaching and learning. Such awareness (mis)guided my approach to academic research and theological writing. For years, it influenced my understanding of what a "good" paper entails and the criteria and the processes for writing one.

Such awareness also determined the questions I was raising in the writing process as well as the questions I could, and at times refused to, ask. I was reluctant to talk about how my own viewpoints on a given topic may have evolved over the years, partly because of my changing contexts, and what the topic meant for me on a personal level. Consequently, my voice in the paper had to make way for someone else's.

I realized only much later that academic writing, and theological writing in particular, was about something much more profound and meaningful than meeting the expectations of others, teachers included. Part of this realization was that I was writing, or at least that I should be writing, for my own learning, edification, and spiritual growth as much as I write for others. It was a liberating realization in many ways, and it changed my approach to writing, the questions I ask, and my expectations of the process.

Writing, Reflection, and Self-Discovery

We who write often hear how important it can be to learn about our intended audience. As a writer, gaining adequate knowledge of my potential readers, their contexts, lived experiences, worldviews, and assumptions can be immensely helpful in shaping my writing so as to make it more intelligible and accessible to them. It can also help make my work more relevant for the needs of my readers and allow me to build bridges to them and connect with them on a deeper level. Such bridge building can in turn facilitate a more effective communication of my ideas.

The writing process, however, is not solely about knowing one's potential readers and connecting with them. A deep knowledge of one's own self is equally important for those who take writing seriously. Such knowledge can be gained from an intentional and keen reflection on your contexts, lived experiences, standing in society, and stances on various issues. Such knowledge can positively expose your worldview, biases, and preconceived notions about the subject matter and possibly also about the reader's own predetermined notions. Good writing requires that the writers begin by reflecting on themselves, on the subject matter, and on the self in relation to that subject matter. This reflection can enable writers to connect with themselves on a deeper level vis-à-vis the subject matter and to become aware of their preconceived notions and biases as they seek to relate to readers.

Reflection on your own self in all its various dimensions certainly has the potential to make you a better writer and communicator. But this relationship between self-reflection and writing works the other way as well. Just as reflection on the self, especially in relation to the subject matter, can contribute to better writing, the writing process itself can offer great means of reflection on yourself, often in relation to the subject matter. While writing papers, seminary students should approach assignments as opportunities for reflections not only about the subject matter but also about themselves. It is important to ask what your writing (the content) says about you and what your writing practices reveal about your values and commitments. Furthermore, it is worth asking how what you write, as well as your practice of writing, might contribute to your own growth as an individual.

My experience with writing has been that it offers an opportunity to reflect and to be in dialogue with myself in ways that can make me more aware of my various environments and intellectual leanings as well as the viewpoints of authors who have influenced me. Writing can become an intense dialogue that reveals a great deal about our theological, intellectual, and ideological assumptions as writers. It can clarify for the writer both the subject matter and her or his own thought process regarding it. Such self-discovery becomes possible only if you are willing to ask tough questions of yourself, of the subject matter at hand, and of your viewpoints on the subject matter. It also requires you to have the ability to address the questions on various levels with intellectual honesty and the courage to be open about what emerges.

In short, writing can provide a great opportunity to learn about yourself. In this scenario, self-reflection is not (just) the *means* to better writing but the *end*. The writing process is the means that can lead to enhanced self-awareness. The relationship between self-reflection leading to self-discovery and the process of writing can be intricate and helpfully symbiotic.

Writing as Dialogue

Any writing process that has been given sufficient attention can facilitate a three-way conversation. As I suggested above, writing is partly about the writer making a connection with the readers. It is also about getting to know your audience and letting them know about you in an intellectual, personal, and spiritual way. In authoring an article or a book, a writer invites the readers—intentionally or unintentionally—into his or her intellectual and spiritual space in ways that facilitate a conversation between them. There is a certain degree of boundary crossing that can serve as a catalyst for intense dialogues between the author and the readers. Good writing often also entails in-depth conversations with the authors who find a place in one's writing. In this sense, it is essential that the writer treat the subject matter, the readers, and the authors who find a mention in the book as dialogue partners in the writing process.

Mikhail Bakhtin, a Russian literary critic and philosopher, describes writing as primarily having a dialogic component to it. Bakhtin, who sees any writing or speech as participation in a continuum of communication, suggests that "any utterance is a link in the chain of communication."[1] In his view, writing is, at its core, an act of being in dialogue and communion with others, especially with the intellectual predecessors who have gone before us. Writing is also an act of engaging those who might come after us in dialogue as we anticipate their participation in the conversation.

This dialogic aspect of writing, and its emphasis, has a profoundly spiritual dimension. It entails opening up of spaces—literally or metaphorically—to others, inviting them to enter, and crossing boundaries that can lead to a new level of familiarity. Before you can open up your intellectual, spiritual spaces and invite others into them, a level of trust is required. Conversely, those entering these spaces must also express a certain level of trust. Both parties express a willingness and a certain amount of courage to expose themselves to encounters that can be enriching and stimulating, but at times also potentially uncomfortable.

Writing is one way to stay connected to others with similar interests and worldviews. Good writing also places a writer in a conversation with others, with all their otherness and divergent viewpoints, in ways that can lead to some life-changing dialogues. I have found that such conversations with others challenge me, force me to clarify and rearticulate my thoughts, and sharpen my thinking on the subject matter. These conversations shape my ideas and allow me to grow in many ways. Writing is a deeply intellectual, spiritual exercise that takes place in communion with others and in mutuality. Similarly, in the process of writing, I am often shaped and changed

1. Mikhail Bakhtin, *Speech Genres and Other Late Essays* (Austin: University of Texas Press, 1986), 84.

by my writing even before it has the opportunity to challenge and shape anyone else. There is a certain level of mutuality and symbiosis in such writing. The writer enhances the piece he or she writes, and, in turn, it enhances the writer.

Bakhtin's concept of writing is also partly about actively accommodating multiple perspectives in your writing. Bakhtin juxtaposes the novels of Dostoevsky with those of Tolstoy to make a distinction between monologic and dialogic novels. He considers Tolstoy's novels to be monologic, because, although the writing contains multiple voices, one voice—that of the author—usually dominates the conversation. In his view, Dostoevsky's novels, such as *The Brothers Karamazov*, are dialogic as they accommodate divergent voices and facilitate a dialogue between them without privileging any one voice at the expense of the rest.[2] Bakhtin suggests that making room for divergent voices is a key characteristic of a dialogic novel, which, on some level, relies on these many viewpoints for its very existence. When applied to theological, academic papers, the concept of dialogic writing introduces readers to multiple, competing perspectives and allows readers to reflect on them and arrive at their own conclusions. Such a dialogic approach to writing implies a level of respect not only for the various voices that underlie multiple perspectives but also for readers themselves.

A theological implication also inhabits that approach, as it suggests that multiple, competing voices can coexist in literary and real, intellectual and theological spaces. Furthermore, it envisions a truth that not only accommodates multiple perspectives but actually requires more than one perspective for it to be authentic. This kind of dialogic approach and writing also has an ethical dimension. With its emphasis on making room for divergent perspectives with all

2. Mikhail Bakhtin, *Problems of Dostoevksy's Poetics* (Minneapolis: University of Minnesota Press, 1993).

their multiplicities and theological and ideological varieties, a dialogic piece of writing can serve as a possible model for how one should approach real life contexts that are characterized by competing worldviews.

Writing as a Transformative Experience

Writing in general, and theological writing in particular, is not just about the mechanics of producing a paper or how you shape it or what kind of paper emerges at the end of the process. It is also about the impact the process might have on the person writing the paper. It is about how writing can affect and transform you. Your interpretation of Scripture, for instance, has the potential to affect your readers, but how can the practice of writing also shape and affect you, the writer? How does writing theologically change your perception of Scripture and your relationship with it?

The French philosopher Paul Ricoeur describes discourse and, by extension, text as an event.[3] He is primarily interested in how spoken discourse functions, but his insights apply to a written text as well. Part of his insight is that a text is not a passive entity but an event that can facilitate interaction with those outside it. In writing, text as an event moves in at least two trajectories. It is an event that is geared toward the readers, but it is also geared toward the self. The event has both an outward and an inward trajectory, which can affect the writer significantly.

A student who took my course Postcolonial Readings of the New Testament recently reported a similarly transformative experience. He signed up for the class primarily because he was curious about this new methodology and because the course fit his schedule well.

3. Paul Ricoeur, *From Text to Action: Essays in Hermeneutics 2*, trans. Kathleen Blamey and John B. Thompson (Evanston, IL: Northwestern University Press, 1986), 77–82.

And yet, as he admitted at the outset, he was "not entirely sure of the course's agenda." During class discussions the first few weeks, he was quite resistant to new readings and to any suggestion that empire and colonialism permeate most books of the Bible. Things changed after he decided to write a research paper on the portrayal of Roman officials in the book of Acts. In writing the paper, he encountered ideas that were not much different from what we discussed in class. As it turns out, however, he was much less resistant to those ideas while writing the paper than in class. His views on empire in the Bible changed radically, resulting in a new, more mature way of relating to Scriptures. Over the years, I have had students who have experienced similar transformations through classroom conversations. This student, however, was more open to such conversations and change in his writing process than in classroom discussion. It appears that he felt far more comfortable allowing himself to be more open (and less guarded) in his personal engagement with biblical texts and with books on the subject. More important, he allowed the writing process, as well as the various interactions therein, to transform him.

Such transformative experience can be quite rewarding in the life of ministry. This is not so much to suggest that students should seek joy in writing papers but that they should seek out the positive aspects of writing and learn how writing can liberate them in many ways. If one takes the writing process seriously, it can free the writer of her or his biases and preconceived notions about the subject matter. It can also reveal the extent to which one's own contexts and life experiences influence the way he or she relates to the subject matter. Consequently, one would be in a better position to understand, if not endorse, others who hold to contrary viewpoints.

Intense, reflective writing that faithfully engages the subject matter (Scripture, in this case) can affect you in life-changing ways. For that to happen, you need the courage to write honestly, rigorously, and faithfully. You need courage to let your own engagement with the subject matter affect you. You need patience to delve deep into texts and ask tough, uncomfortable questions, both of the subject matter and of yourself. Be in conversation with your writing and turn it into a dialogue partner, allowing it to have its own voice so it can speak back to you. Allow your authors—your conversation partners—as well as your own writing to challenge you intellectually and spiritually. In my experience with students, what emerges as a result of an honest dialogue with the texts is no longer a naïve or unchallenged relationship with Scriptures but a more mature and grounded relationship. The same applies to our relationship with our traditions and other long-held ideas.

The discipline of writing need not be primarily about producing a well-crafted composition. Although that might be part of the process, to a great extent, theological writing pertains to one's active engagement with the text and to what emerges as a result of the interaction. You come to a text with your own hopes, biases, viewpoints, and boundaries, all of which are limited and limiting. You make yourself vulnerable, or at least you ought to, in front of the texts and honest with them so that texts and interaction with them can have transforming effects. The practice of writing is as much about what happens in the engagement as it is about the piece that emerges out of the interaction. As Michel Foucault helpfully observed, writing can transform "the things seen or heard 'into tissue and blood' (*in vires et in sanguinem*). It becomes a principle of rational action in the writer himself."[4]

When taken seriously, your writing can affect the self in truly liberating ways before it can affect anyone else. For this to happen,

---

4. Michel Foucault, *Ethics: Subjectivity and Truth* (New York: New Press, 1998), 213.

your writing process needs to take on a life of its own. You need to allow some liberty for what is being written so that it can, in turn, liberate the one writing it. For the writing process to be transformative, aim to strike a balance between being immersed in the writing and distancing yourself from it so that it might transform and shape you.

The writing process challenges the self, expands your horizons, and alters the way you view the world, how you relate to others and to the subject matter. Writing can help you explore the subject matter as well as the self. You explore the subject matter in light of your background and in the context of your worldview. In a similar vein, you explore the self in relation to the subject matter as well as its ideologies, assumptions, and biases. The writer's biases and worldviews shape her or his writing and transform the subject matter, but, in turn, that which is written also affects and shapes the writer. The process can be mutually enriching and transformative.

With such mutual transformation in mind, it is important for you to choose topics that can have a shaping effect, aid spiritual growth, and expand intellectual horizons. Try to identify in each paper aspects that can offer opportunities and avenues for deep spiritual reflection beyond the academic research, and pay keen attention to such aspects. Spiritual reflection should take place not *instead of* but *alongside* rigorous academic research for the paper. Finally, identify topics and assignments that may have aroused your intellectual curiosity in significant ways and challenged you to move beyond your comfort zone. Make it a point to return to them at a later point and engage them, perhaps once you enter ministry. This takes a great deal of intentionality and discipline, but the rewards of such reflective writing will be significant. Given the daily demands of ministry, it can be easy to lose track of your spiritual and intellectual needs, but revisiting topics of interest can facilitate your own edification, expand horizons of understanding, and provide opportunities for reflecting on your own intellectual, spiritual journey. It can also enhance your ability to relate to, and engage, those with similar intellectual interests, including parishioners.

Writing as Contemplation

Beyond writing research papers to fulfill academic requirements, I would invite you to undertake reflective writing in ways that will have significant and lasting benefits for your personal and spiritual life. Writing should be seen not just as an assignment for a course or as a short-term practice that helps you complete the degree but rather as a sustained, long-term practice that will provide the spiritual edification and intellectual growth required of anyone wanting to minister in congregations. Given this long-term dimension of writing, it is important to develop habits and practices that will sustain you throughout your vocation. To develop techniques for engaging papers in such way that the focus shifts from the purely academic to the contemplative mode, find environments and writing practices that can lend themselves to such contemplation. One such practice pertains to carving out sufficient time and the right kind of space for writing, space that will allow you to reflect spiritually in addition to thinking critically. Explore ways to carve out intellectual and personal space for intentional, contemplative, and creative writing. It is important to find spaces that will enable you to be creative, to reflect, to express yourself, and to be transformed in the process of writing. Different places and spaces function differently for different people. At the same time, the same person might need different types of spaces for different kinds of writing and at different stages of writing. Open spaces work well for some, but others might prefer closed spaces. Some seek out open spaces during earlier stages of working on a project, but they might work better in closed spaces during later stages of writing.

Develop writing practices that can be sustaining and positively challenging. Try to re-envision writing in ways that can meet your needs on many levels. The key is to explore different ways of writing and to experiment with different locations and strategies to see what proves to be the most rewarding in offering personal reflection and spiritual growth. Be open to new ideas that might surprise you in wonderful ways and nourish you. Since words have power, play with words and language in ways that might feed your soul and facilitate spiritual growth.

Writing can be a process of intense spiritual reflection that fosters intellectual and spiritual growth. This growth, however, requires an intentionality and imagination that allows writers to envision writing for themselves before they write for others. Such an imagination enables writers to position themselves as keen readers and honest critics of their own writing. This approach to writing for the self and the resultant self-reflection forces one to question his or her own viewpoints and assumptions about the subject matter and to achieve clarity about oneself before the self is extended to others through the written work.

After all, each of us truly knows our self only to the extent we discover it. Writing is a form of art that is often the best medium for such a discovery. As Michel Foucault aptly observed, "From the idea that the self is not given to us, I think that there is only one practical consequence: we have to create ourselves as a work of art."[5]

---

5. Michel Foucault, *Michel Foucault: Beyond Structuralism and Hermeneutics*, ed. Hubert L. Dreyfus and P. Rabinow, 2nd ed. (Chicago: University of Chicago Press, 1983), 237.

10

Writing Spiritually

Jacob D. Myers

Just in case nobody's told you yet, allow me to let you in on an ineluctable consequence of pursuing a seminary education.

You. Will. Write. A lot!

Writing is to the seminarian what plowing is to the farmer; it may feel like painful, backbreaking work, but without it "don't nothin' grow," as they say in my neck of the woods.

Now, I know what you're thinking. You just finished reading a dozen or so essays en route to learning how to write theologically, and here you find this essay on writing spiritually— tacked on at the end, little more than an afterthought. It's that thing you'll attend to if you have time, once all your other work is complete. Yet, unlike this essay, your spirituality is not something to get to when you have time, because you will never *have* time. You must *take* time. But where does one *find* the time when seminary already feels like an all-you-can-eat hotdog competition? Amidst Hebrew vocab lists, Greek paradigm charts, and troves of history and theology to read, what room is left for spiritual consumption?

I'll show you, but you'll have to be willing to be a bit sneaky. Are you ready?

To begin, you should know that I'm writing as someone who has been where you are now. I want to help you see that writing spiritually is far more than writing prayers, devotionals, or sermons. If you follow me through this essay, I'll show you how *all writing* can become spiritual writing; in fact, it already is. I will help you to view your myriad précis, reflection papers, and essays to be less like hoops you must jump through in route to graduation and more like opportunities for spiritual invigoration.

Genus *Spiritualis*

To proceed, we must remove the dross surrounding the concept of spirituality. As Lucy Bregman aptly observes in *The Ecology of Spirituality*, the words *spirituality* and *spiritual* are so ubiquitous that they have come to mean almost anything one wants them to. It is unclear, for instance, whether one *has* spirituality or whether spirituality is something one *attains*. Some see spirituality as intrinsic to Christian faith and praxis, and others view it as a threat.[1] So what do we mean when we talk about writing spiritually?

Ecclesiologist Tony Jones gets spirituality right when he observes, "No matter one's theological disposition, it's clear the protagonist in the relationship is God."[2] For Jones, as well as myself, a proper understanding of spirituality flows from this God-centered

1. Lucy Bregman, *The Ecology of Spirituality: Meanings, Virtues, and Practices in a Post-Religious Age* (Waco, TX: Baylor University Press, 2013), 41.
2. Tony Jones, *The Sacred Way: Spiritual Practices for Everyday Life* (Grand Rapids: Zondervan, 2005), 26.

commitment, which is informed most concretely by Swiss theologian Karl Barth. It is a view of spirituality that resists a radically withdrawn, me-and-my-Jesus orientation *as well as* a human-centered we-can-save-the-world-all-by-ourselves approach.[3] For Barth, spirituality marks the "special movement and act of God in the work of the Holy Spirit" in and through the thoughts *and actions* of Christ followers, and as such, it is only loosely related to religiosity.[4] The spiritual transcends the mundane, even the mundanity of religious and theological discourse. Therefore, we

3. See Karl Barth, "Jesus Christ and the Movement of Social Justice (1911)," in *Karl Barth and Radical Politics*, ed. George Hunsinger (Philadelphia: Westminster, 1976), 19–46, and "Past and Future: Friedrich Naumann and Christoph Blumhardt," in *The Beginnings of Dialectic Theology*, vol. 1, ed. James M. Robinson, trans. Keith R. Crim (Richmond, VA: John Knox, 1968), 36: "There is an uncomfortable moment when an upright man begins to reflect with both open eyes about religion and about life. Religion? Yes, what does religion mean and what help is it; what is the truth of religion when life with its ordinances and relationships, the whole raging course of the world as it is, so notoriously bypasses the love and righteousness of God, of which religion speaks?" Or, as he puts it later, in his *Evangelical Theology: An Introduction*, trans. Foley Grover (Grand Rapids: Eerdmans, 1963), 78:

> This Word concerns mankind [sic] in all times and places, the theologian in his own time and place, and the world in its occupation with the routine Problems of the everyday. This Word challenges the world in which X, Y, and Z appear—with their own big words—to have the say and to determine the lot of all men and things as well as the lot of theologians. While the theologian reads the newspaper, he [sic] cannot forget that he has just read Isaiah 40 or John 1 or Romans 8. He, at any rate, cannot suppress the knowledge that the Word of God speaks not only of an infinitely deeper need but also of an infinitely higher promise than the sum total of all the needs and promises characteristic of his time and place.

4. Karl Barth, *The Christian Life: Church Dogmatics* vol. 4, pt. 4. *Lecture Fragments*, trans. Geoffrey W. Bromiley (Grand Rapids: Eerdmans, 1981), 92:

> In modern usage the term "spiritual" has wrongly been put in embarrassing proximity to the word "religious." It should be related to this word only indirectly and not very firmly. What has been forgotten is that, among Christians at least, the word "spiritual" can denote only a new definition of the human spirit, of the whole of this spirit, by the Holy Spirit, so that it cannot refer to a variation or modification of human spiritual activity as such. *Geistlich* and *geistig*, which, unfortunately, like *Geschichte* and *Historie*, can be distinguished linguistically only in German, denote two different things. *Geistig* denotes the capacity for orientation to something transcendent, and it thus implies a religious life in some sense and to some degree. But in the use of this capacity, what is *geistig* is not necessarily *geistlich*. The *geistlich* has contacts with it. It operates in its sphere. It uses its possibilities. It determines, controls, and penetrates it. Yet it has and retains its own individuality, distinctiveness, and movement in relation to the religious life as well as the scientific, moral, political, and aesthetic life. It has no special affinity to the religious life.

could say that all seminary writing is inherently *theological* but that not all seminary writing is necessarily *spiritual*. Let's talk about how we can change that.

The Spirituality of Discourse

Writing is a spiritual enterprise because it draws the individual into the matrix of language, which is socially constructed. And again, I'm not just talking about devotional literature or written prayers. *Every* act of writing constitutes a spiritual decision: you either open yourself to the "dominion of the Spirit," as Gustavo Gutiérrez puts it, or you do not.[5] Writing is inherently spiritual because it participates in the two poles of spirituality: the personal and the sociopolitical.

Every act of discourse is inherently political. It is never neutral. As discourse, writing is inseparable from systems of power and privilege to which you either acquiesce or resist. Likewise, your spirituality is inextricable from your politics (Prov. 21:13; Phil. 2:4; 1 John 3:17). If you accede to the governing powers and principalities—that is, the structures that legitimate and perpetuate violence and marginalization against some people while offering preferential treatment to others—then you participate in your own spiritual poverty.

On the other hand, a person can engage writing as a means to spiritual liberation. What this means is that the writer, recognizing the sociopolitical entanglements of her discourse, employs writing to liberate marginalized others and to exhort the powers and

5. Gustavo Gutiérrez, *A Theology of Liberation: History, Politics, and Salvation*, ed. and trans. Caridad Inda and John Eagleson, 15th anniversary ed. (Maryknoll, NY: Orbis Books, 1988), 117: "Spirituality, in the strict and profound sense of the word, is the dominion of the Spirit that transforms every detail of our lives, . . . [who] will lead us to complete freedom, the freedom from everything that hinders us from fulfilling ourselves as human beings and offspring of God, and the freedom to love and to enter into community with God and with others."

principalities to set people free—even yourself, even in seminary. "This is a spirituality that dares to sink roots in the soil of oppression and germinate the seeds of liberation."[6] Writing can facilitate such a spirituality.

We can, and we will through the course of this essay, flip this equation around. All discourse is inherently spiritual, *and* all spirituality is inherently discursive. Spirituality is structured like writing; it is made possible by the *necessary gap* between the self and God, the self and others, even the self with the self. Because spirituality and writing both participate in and are grounded by a certain otherness, they each open a path toward a way of thinking that calls into question the governing assumptions of systems of thought. This is also known as deconstruction, which is another word for justice.[7]

Writing *Spiritually*

What does it mean to write *spiritually*? Said differently, what does it mean to write in such a way that the *truly spiritual* is able to shine through our *religious* discourse? As we move forward, let me be clear: first, writing, even *spiritual* writing, cannot guarantee union with the Divine. Writing functions as a summons. It opens a generative space where God can work in and through our words and according to God's good pleasure transform them into *God's* Word. Second, writing *spiritually* is not a one-size-fits-all program. Let me explain.

6. Gustavo Gutiérrez, *Spiritual Writings*, ed. Daniel G. Groody (Maryknoll, NY: Orbis Books, 2011), 47.
7. See Jacques Derrida, "Force of Law: The 'Mystical Foundation of Authority,'" in *Deconstruction and the Possibility of Justice*, ed. David Gray Carlson, Drucilla Cornell, and Michel Rosenfeld (London: Rutledge, 1992), 3–67.

Writing *spiritually* relates differently to marginalized people than to people who are born into positions of power and privilege. It is incumbent upon those of us who are born into power and privilege to employ our discourse in the service of liberation. This requires a *conversion* to human and nonhuman others, a striving to open oneself to the lived experiences of other people and a *yearning* to seek justice on their behalf. Such is the mantle of responsibility placed upon those with power and privilege (Luke 18:18-25). For such—which I myself am as an educated, white, straight, American male—it is imperative that we divest ourselves of our power positions in order to create space for the other. Jon Sobrino writes about such divestment as a *political holiness* that conjoins with a kind of sociopolitical ascesis or self-divestment. Not unlike the Christian concept of *kenosis*, people like me must willfully strip themselves of power in order to "denounce and unmask oppression."[8]

Obversely, those who are marginalized on account of their race, ethnicity, sexual orientation, or gender may use their writing to liberate not only themselves but also others who share their struggles. The boldness of deconstruction is just as much of a spiritual act for marginalized persons as divestment is for those with power.

We need not strain to witness the spiritual fervor emerging from the voices of those writing from societies' margins. For instance, observe how novelist and playwright Pearl Cleage captures the two poles of spirituality—the personal and the sociopolitical—in her introductory essay to *Mad at Miles*:

---

8. Jon Sobrino, *Spirituality of Liberation: Toward Political Holiness*, trans. Robert R. Barr (Maryknoll, NY: Orbis Books, 1988), 82. N.b., Kenosis is troubled by feminist scholarship and the recent contributions by scholars like Anna Mercedes, *Power For: Feminism and Christ's Self-Giving* (London: T & T Clark, 2011), draw our attention to the power arising from such acts as a power "that leans toward others and offers itself to them" (7). Such "power for" the other can actually lead to human flourishing rather than further subjugating and silencing already marginalized bodies and voices.

I am writing to expose and explore the point where racism and sexism meet. I am writing to help understand the full effects of being black and female in a culture that is both racist and sexist. I am writing to try and communicate that information to my sisters first and then to any brothers of goodwill and honest intent who will take the time to listen. . . . I am writing to allow myself to feel the anger. I am writing to keep from running toward it or away from it or into anybody's arms. I am writing to find solutions and pass them on. I am writing to find a language and pass it on. I am writing, writing, writing, for my life.[9]

This is how I want you to write in seminary, to write as if your life depended on it, for your transformation ought not begin at graduation but at matriculation.

At base, *spiritual* discourse—speech as well as writing—demands that we write out of our lived experience, and this is something that may encounter resistance from some of your seminary professors. Do not succumb. Do not allow the academic powers and principalities to stifle your spiritual development, your movement toward political holiness. Embrace who you are. Name your privilege along with your pain. Novelist Flannery O'Connor once explained, "I write the way I do because and only because I am a Catholic. I feel that if I were not a Catholic, I would have no reason to write, no reason to see, no reason ever to feel horrified or even enjoy anything."[10] Like O'Connor, you should write out of your lived experience and theological commitments.

Spiritual writing arises out of what Sobrino labels a "*spiritual mentality*—not because 'spiritual' means pure interiority here, as opposed to history, but because it is the fruit and expression of the Spirit; and it is the Spirit that time and again proposes the ideal,

---

9. Pearl Cleage, excerpted from *Deals with the Devil: And Other Reasons to Riot*, in *The New Georgia Encyclopedia Companion to Georgia Literature*, ed. Hugh Ruppersburg (Athens: University of Georgia Press, 2007), 85.
10. Flannery O'Connor, "Letter to John Lynch, November 6, 1955," in *Flannery O'Connor: Spiritual Writings*, ed. Robert Ellsberg (Maryknoll, NY: Orbis Books, 2003), 126.

refusing to let us strike a compromise with the factual."[11] Likewise, in his book *We Drink from Our Own Wells*, Gutiérrez writes about the importance of grounding one's spirituality in one's lived experience. He urges his Latin American sisters and brothers to lean into the pain and atrocities they have experienced, because out of them a "new spirituality" is emerging. Such is a "new and different way of following Jesus, . . . different means proper to Latin America and shaped by the real experiences of the Latin American countries."[12] Such new spiritualities can take root in your writing, no matter your particular context. What makes the difference is your writing's orientation around questions of justice and righteousness and love wherever you are.

Writing *spiritually*—that is, writing in such a way that you open yourself up to God's empowering presence and to the world that God loves—will keep the fires of faith burning brightly within you. If you can learn to write spiritually, you will leave seminary more rather than less excited about, committed to, and shaped by your calling to serve God than when you matriculated.

My own writing—even my academic writing, even this essay—is intrinsic to my spiritual development. When I write, I allow those thoughts and emotions that abide on the periphery of my consciousness to meld with what I hear and read. I allow the otherness that as a white, straight male I could hold at bay if I chose. When I write, I enter a world that is at once my own and not my own. In such a world, I am exposed, and I make myself vulnerable to the other, including the Divine Other. In this regard, my perspective on writing is similar to the French historian and philosopher Michel Foucault. In his book *The Archaeology of Knowledge*, Foucault delves

---

11. Sobrino, *Spirituality of Liberation*, 39.
12. Gustavo Gutiérrez, *We Drink from Our Own Wells: The Spiritual Journey of a People*, trans. Matthew J. O'Connell (Maryknoll, NY: Orbis Books, 2003), 25.

into questions of the human being, consciousness, the origin of thought, and the emergence of the subject. He asks,

> What, do you imagine that I would take so much pleasure in writing, do you think that I would keep so persistently to my task, if I were not preparing—with a rather shaky hand—a labyrinth into which I can venture, in which I can move my discourse, opening up underground passages, forcing it to go far from itself, finding overhangs that reduce and deform its itinerary, in which I can lose myself and appear at last to eyes that I will never have to meet again.[13]

Like Foucault, I write to lose myself; but I also write to find myself, before God and neighbor; indeed, it is only in losing ourselves before the other that we find ourselves in God.

Theological writing constructs a spiritual labyrinth, and it is in such a labyrinth that you will discover those "underground passages" that open you up to the constructed power structures that govern your life. When you can name those structures, you can begin to unname them, which is another way of talking about deconstruction. Writing theologically *can be* spiritual writing. But this requires a certain temperament, a certain epistemological approach, and it is this that I desire for you to know.

Writing *spiritually* is a risky, even perilous endeavor. When you write about history or lobster fishing or professional wrestling or whatever mundane activity, you do not expose yourself to the one who is simultaneously light and yet unlike any light we know (Irenaeus, *Adversus haereses* 2.13.4) and to the other who calls out for justice (Gen. 4:10; Exod. 3:7; Ps. 18:6). *Spiritual* writing is as much a willingness *to be written upon*—where we invite God to incarnate our words, our very souls—as it is a mode of discourse. Writing about

---

13. Michel Foucault, *The Archeology of Knowledge and the Discourse on Language*, trans. A. M. Sheridan Smith (New York: Pantheon Books, 1972), 17.

God inscribes the Divine upon us; it is a spiritual tattoo, of sorts. It participates in the approach of St. Anselm, who writes,

> Come now, O Lord my God. Teach my heart where and how to seek you, where and how to find you. Teach me how to seek you, and show yourself to me when I seek. For I cannot seek you unless you teach me how, and I cannot find you unless you show yourself to me. Let me seek you in desiring you; let me desire you in seeking you. Let me find you in loving you; let me love you in finding you.[14]

When we write about the Divine, we traverse a sacred threshold, one that produces fear and trembling. The greater our power and privilege, the more we ought to tremble.

Writing Spiritually

Let's flip this equation around to discuss the ways in which *writing itself* participates in a certain spirituality. In some ways, all writing is risky business. As Stephen King avers, *you must not come lightly to the blank page*:

> You can approach the act of writing with nervousness, excitement, hopefulness, or even despair—the sense that you can never completely put on the page what's in your heart. You can come to the act with your fists clenched and your eyes narrowed, ready to kick ass and take down names. You can come to it . . . because you want to change the world. Come to it any way but lightly.[15]

Or, as Annie Dillard puts it, writing a book is a bit like sitting up with a dying friend, holding her hand with "dread and sympathy." And, if you skip a visit or two, "a work in progress quickly becomes feral. . . . It is a lion you cage in your study."[16] Writing is a perilous task, and

14. Anselm, *Monologion and Proslogion with the Replies of Gaunilo and Anselm*, trans. Thomas Williams (Indianapolis: Hackett, 1996), 99.
15. Stephen King, *On Writing: A Memoir of the Craft* (New York: Pocket Books, 2000), 99.

we who handle the holy are doubly exposed. We risk our selfhood when we venture to write on things divine.

Okay, you've been warned. Let's move our attention to *writing* as a spiritual act.

How do you *write* spiritually? Before we can answer this question, we have to get a clear understanding of what writing actually is. Against common conceptions, writing is never *just* inscribing thought. Writing is not just a copy of speech. We can think of discourse as the use of signs (whether aural, written, or gestural) that refer to thoughts and concepts. Some suggest that the process of writing corrupts these pure thoughts as they are transferred to paper. If all discourse relies on the use of signs, however, then writing is just one of any number of symbolic tools we can use.[17]

All writing—along with all speech—participates in a certain absence that is necessary for all forms of signification. For example, inscribing the letter *B* is only meaningful as a letter that evokes a certain sound in your mind when we understand that letter as one of twenty-six others that make up the English alphabet. Therefore, the *B*-ness of the letter *B* receives and retains something from all the other letters of the alphabet that are at once absent but not completely absent because their presence is necessary to structure the sound and meaning that *B* makes. There is no *necessary* reason why the letter *B* should signify the sound that it does. As English users we submit to this convention, agreeing to let *B* signify in a certain way.

16. Annie Dillard, *The Writing Life* (New York: Harper & Row, 1989), 52.
17. Jacques Derrida, "Semiology and Grammatology: An Interview with Julia Kristeva," in *Positions*, trans. Alan Bass (Chicago: University of Chicago Press, 1982), 22: "The exteriority of the signifier seems reduced. Naturally this experience is a lure, but a lure whose necessity has organized an entire structure, or an entire epoch; and on the ground of this epoch a semiology has been constituted whose concepts and fundamental presuppositions are quite precisely discernable from Plato to Husserl, passing through Aristotle, Rousseau, Hegel, etc."

(I know this is getting philosophically heavy, but stick with it. This is so important.)

In this way, we can think of writing as constructed out of what scholars call a socio-symbolic matrix of language. This means that writing emerges out of an absence, a spacing, that is necessary for communication with other people. To employ discourse to communicate in our writing, we plug into this matrix so that our marks on the page—*writing*—can signify our thoughts. So, given this understanding of language as a mode of signification sustained by cultures and symbols (letters), writing can facilitate a certain spirituality that French philosopher Jacques Derrida labels "deconstruction." Put simply, deconstruction points a finger (you decide which one) to the constructed nature of language and to the otherness that is excluded in order to render meaning through language, asking, "What about the other?"

Here's a concrete example of what I'm talking about.

A whole host of commitments are wrapped up in the designation *male*. Deconstruction says, "Wait a minute, guys. Could we have the concept 'male' without the concept 'female' to structure it? Not really. And furthermore, how come our society tends to privilege 'male' over 'female' when the latter is necessary for the former? Maybe it doesn't have to be that way." Deconstruction can foster our spirituality by allowing us to point to the cracks and fissures plastered over by centuries of philosophical and theological spackle. It can set your spirit free from the cage of language by enabling you to interrogate the philosophical commitments always already entwined with language.[18] It can call for justice.

18. As Derrida observes, "The movements of deconstruction do not destroy structures from the outside. They are not possible and effective, nor can they take accurate aim, except by inhabiting those structures. Inhabiting them *in a certain way*, because one always inhabits, and all the more when one does not suspect it." *Of Grammatology*, trans. Gayatri Chakravorty Spivak, corrected ed. (Baltimore: The Johns Hopkins University Press, 1997), 24. This is

A writing that participates in a certain deconstruction is not just writing, but neither can it be conflated with the Spirit's agency. Rather, I believe that a writing oriented to deconstruction *points* to the arbitrary and differential structure of language from within language, and that such *pointing* works to liberate the created order toward the freedom inaugurated by the Holy Spirit. To employ Barth's language, deconstruction is a kind of *geistig* (human capacity or orientation) that creates space—hospitality, hospice—for the *geistlich*, the truly spiritual; by pointing to the shaky foundations of our theological, political, and social structures, it makes room for the Spirit to do her liberative work. Nevertheless, when we direct our writing to the liberation of oppressed human and nonhuman others, we cannot help but experience, as Barth describes in his *Epistle to the Romans*, the "shattering disturbance" that "brings everything into question."[19]

Such a mode of *writing* spiritually also participates in the liberative agency inaugurated by the Word of God revealed in Scripture, whose fullest likeness we encounter in the life and ministry of Jesus. As theologian Rebecca Chopp notes in *The Power to Speak*, the Word signifies an alternative order beyond all significations that are a part of the present order of domination and injustice.[20] Said

not a "radical rupture and discontinuity" that some criticize. See Andreas Huyssen, *After the Great Divide: Modernism, Mass Culture, Postmodernism* (Bloomington: Indiana University Press, 1986), 207. In his essay, "The Ends of Man," in *Margins of Philosophy*, trans. Alan Bass (Chicago: University of Chicago Press, 1982), 134-5, Derrida differentiates between a *trembling* and a *radical trembling*: "A radical trembling can only come from the *outside*. Therefore, the trembling of which I speak derives no more than any other from some spontaneous decision or philosophical thought after some internal maturation of its history."

19. Karl Barth, *Epistle to the Romans*, trans. Edwyn C. Hoskyns, 6th ed. (London: Oxford University Press, 1933), 225.

20. Rebecca Chopp, *The Power To Speak: Feminism, Language, God* (New York: Crossroads, 1989). By pointing to the underlying philosophical constructs—in language, subjectivity, and politics—that fund both Christian theology proper and feminist theologies, Chopp troubles the foundation upon which theology rests. Such a project is motivated by a Protestant theological conviction and a feminist ideological principle, both of which call for liberation. She writes,

differently, the liberative kingdom inaugurated by Jesus' reign is already deconstructing the present order. Chopp gets it right when she declares that the Word is radically free and is therefore not subject to the political, linguistic, and even theological constrains thrust upon the Word. We might think of the Word as a free safety in football: free to roam and to run its own routes and eager to halt the progress of the opponent. *Writing* spiritually participates in the liberative agency of the Word. As such, it can free us from the ecclesial prisons constructed by patriarchal, ethnocentric, and heteronormative forces and thereby pronounce emancipatory transformation for the whole world.

Or consider the writing of James Cone, who melds the liberative and the spiritual with poetic potency. In *The Cross and the Lynching Tree*, Cone writes,

> Though we are not fully free and the dream not fully realized, yet, *we are not what we used to be and not what we will be*. The cross and the lynching tree can help us to know from where we have come and where we must go. We continue to seek an ultimate meaning that cannot be expressed in rational and historical language and that cannot be denied by white supremacy. Poetry is often more helpful than prose in expressing our hope. Through poetic imagination we can see the God of Jesus revealed in the cross and the lynching tree. Those who saw this connection more clearly than others were artists, poets, and writers.[21]

What if you thought of your writing opportunities in seminary as a means of honing such a "poetic imagination" within you? Think of

"Women will be forever strangers unless their words and their voices revise the social and symbolic rules of language, transforming the law of ordered hierarchy in language, in subjectivity, and in politics into a grace of rich plenitude for human flourishing" (2).

21. James H. Cone, *The Cross and the Lynching Tree* (Maryknoll, NY: Orbis Books, 2011), 92. This book can be read as a form of spiritual lament and theological protest, both of which writing spiritually summon. With Cone, the cross and the lynching tree are symbols that inaugurate a certain trembling in American—and especially white—theology. They call forth a "hope beyond tragedy" (166) and a cruciform imagination that deconstructs "one's own social reality" (158).

what kind of minister you could become if you attuned your vision and sharpened your quill to an "ultimate meaning" beyond rational thought and language? May God grant us such vision!

Writing Spiritually

There is only one way to write spiritually, and that is with your whole being attuned to the God of justice and peace who shatters oppressive systems and who furtively inaugurates God's kingdom like a woman smuggling yeast into a measure of flour (Matt. 13:33). Altering Meister Eckhart's words slightly we read: "We ought to [write] so powerfully that we should like to put our every member and strength, our two eyes and ears, mouth, heart and all our senses to work; and we should not give up until we find that we wish to be one with [the One] who is present to us and whom we entreat, namely God."[22] Cone's words are no less true for the seminarian who would endeavor to *write spiritually*: "To know the truth is to appropriate it, for it is not mainly reflection and theory. Truth is divine action entering into our lives and creating the human action of liberation. Truth enables us to dance and live to the rhythm of freedom in our lives as we struggle to be who we are."[23]

Writing with your whole being is not a painless task. Not for anybody. If you were born into structures of privilege on account of your race, ethnicity, sexual orientation, or gender, then writing spiritually might feel a bit like Harry Potter felt when he was forced to write with Professor Umbridge's blood quill. To write in such a way that you acknowledge your sociopolitical advantages can cut

22. Meister Eckhart, "Counsels on Discernment," in *Meister Eckhart: The Essential Sermons, Commentaries, Treatises, and Defense,* trans. Edmund Colledge and Bernard McGinn (Mawhaw, NJ: Paulist, 1981), 249.
23. James H. Cone, *God of the Oppressed,* rev. ed. (Maryknoll, NY: Orbis Books, 1997), 28.

deeply. That's why we must attend carefully to the writings of those who have not shared our same entitlements. Know that such writing will make you a better minister and a stronger Christian. I bear witness to this.

For men and women who have been denied power and agency, seminary will be painful but in a different way. You must write out of and into that pain, fighting to deconstruct those systems of power that silence and subjugate you and others like you who do not have the opportunity to receive a theological education. For you, writing can be a means to liberation—your liberation. As poet Audre Lorde puts it, "Strong women know the taste of their own hatred," they know what it feels like to "always be building nests in a windy place."[24] Unfortunately, these words point to a sad reality. Some theological schools can feel just as unaccommodating as the culture at large. Keep writing. Write in such a way that you can name your pain and thereby experience the divine action entering your life and driving you to the work of liberation.

Let us end by considering a metaphor from Meister Eckhart. *Writing spiritually* is akin to the work of a master sculptor. When such a sculptor makes a figure out of stone, he doesn't introduce the figure *into* the stone. Rather, he cuts away the fragments that had hidden and concealed the figure; he gives nothing to the stone but takes away from it, cutting away its surface and removing its rough covering, and then that which was hidden beneath is able to shine forth.[25] Writing *spiritually* can cut away our rough surfaces—our

---

24. Audre Lorde, "Portrait," in *The Black Unicorn* (New York: Norton, 1978), 51. Or, as she puts it elsewhere, "The quality of light by which we scrutinize our lives has direct bearing upon the product which we live, and upon the changes we hope to bring about through our lives. It is within this light that we form those ideas by which we pursue our magic and make it realized. This is poetry as illumination, for it is through poetry that we give name to those ideas which are—until the poem—nameless and formless, about to be birthed, but already felt." See Audre Lorde, "Poetry Is Not a Luxury," in *Sister Outsider: Essays and Speeches* (New York: Crossing, 2007), 36.

prejudices, ideologies, and assumptions—so that the Spirit who abides within us is able to shine forth.

Yes, in seminary you are expected to master faithful methods of biblical exegesis; the capacity to render ethical, pastoral judgments; and sound techniques of preaching, pastoral care, and liturgical leadership. You are in fact working toward a *Master* of Divinity, are you not? Writing aids our theological development to be sure, but a secret irony is hardwired into our seminary endeavor. We seek to *master* divinity. However, as we matriculate through seminary, we slowly come to realize that the point is not—or, not *only*—to master divinity but to allow the Divine to master *us*. Learning to *write spiritually* fosters such transformation.

25. Meister Eckhart, "The Book of 'Benedictus': Of the Nobleman," in *Meister Eckhart*, 243.

More Writing

This book is only the beginning. When you are ready to reflect more on what it means to write theologically, we commend the following texts to you.

Adler, Mortimer J. and Charles Van Doren. *How to Read a Book*. Rev. ed. New York: Touchstone, 1972.

Apostolos-Cappadona, Diane, ed. *Art, Creativity, and the Sacred: An Anthology in Religion and Art*. New York: Crossroads, 1995.

Bakhtin, M. M. *Speech Genres and Other Late Essays*. Austin, TX: University of Texas Press, 1986.

Caputo, John D. *What Would Jesus Deconstruct: The Good News of Postmodernism for the Church*. The Church and Postmodern Culture. Grand Rapids: Baker Academic, 2007.

Carroll, Brian. *Writing and Editing for Digital Media*. New York: Routledge, 2014.

De La Torre, Miguel and Stacey M. Floyd-Thomas, eds. *Beyond the Pale: Reading Ethics from the Margins*. Louisville, KY: Westminster John Knox, 2011.

Gula, Robert J. *Nonsense: Red Herrings, Straw Men and Sacred Cows: How We Abuse Logic in Our Everyday Language*. Mount Jackson, VA: Axios Press, 2007.

Hacker, Diana and Nancy Sommers. *Writer's Reference*. 7th ed. Boston: Bedford/St. Martin's, 2010.

Kearney, Richard. *On Stories*. Thinking in Action. London: Routledge, 2002.

Lamott, Anne. *Bird by Bird: Some Instructions on Writing and Life*. New York: Anchor, 1995.

McKenzie, Alyce M. *Novel Preaching: Tips from Top Writers for Crafting Creative Sermons*. Louisville, KY: Westminster John Knox, 2010.

Migliore, Daniel L. *Faith Seeking Understanding*. Grand Rapids: Eerdmans, 2004.

Moschella, Mary Clark. *Ethnography as a Pastoral Practice: An Introduction*. Cleveland: Pilgrim, 2008.

National Writing Project. *Because Digital Writing Matters*. San Francisco: Jossey-Bass, 2010.

Sobrino, Jon. *A Spirituality of Liberation: Toward Political Holiness*. Translated by Robert R. Barr. Maryknoll, NY: Orbis, 1988.

Stone, Howard W. and James O. Duke. *How to Think Theologically*. Minneapolis: Augsburg Fortress, 2006.

Trible, Phyllis. *Rhetorical Criticism: Context, Method and the Book of Jonah*. Guides to Biblical Scholarship. Minneapolis: Fortress Press, 1994.

Vrudny, Kimberly and Wilson Yates, eds. *Arts, Theology, and the Church: New Intersections*. Cleveland: Pilgrim, 2005.

Webb, Joseph. *Preaching without Notes*. Nashville: Abingdon, 2001.

Williams, Joseph M. and Gregory G. Colomb. *Style: Lessons in Clarity and Grace*. 10th ed. Boston: Longman, 2010.

Yarber, Angela. *Holy Women Icons*. Cleveland, TN: Parson's Porch Books, 2014.

Bibliography

Althaus-Reid, Marcella. *Indecent Theology: Theological Perversions in Sex, Gender, and Politics.* New York: Routledge, 2000.

Angelou, Maya. *I Know Why the Caged Bird Sings.* New York: Random House, 1969.

Anselm. *Monologion and Proslogion with the Replies of Gaunilo and Anselm.* Translated by Thomas Williams. Indianapolis: Hackett, 1996.

Bakhtin, Mikhail. *Problems of Dostoevsky's Poetics.* Minneapolis: University of Minnesota Press, 1993.

———. *Speech Genres and Other Late Essays.* Austin: University of Texas Press, 1986.

Barth, Karl. *The Christian Life: Church Dogmatics.* Vol. 4, pt. 4, *Lecture Fragments.* Translated by Geoffrey W. Bromiley. Grand Rapids: Eerdmans, 1981.

———. *Epistle to the Romans.* Translated by Edwyn C. Hoskyns. 6th ed. London: Oxford University Press, 1933.

———. *Evangelical Theology: An Introduction.* Translated by Foley Grover. Grand Rapids: Eerdmans, 1963.

———. "Jesus Christ and the Movement of Social Justice (1911)." In *Karl Barth and Radical Politics,* 19–46. Edited by George Hunsinger. Philadelphia: Westminster, 1976.

———. "Past and Future: Friedrich Naumann and Christoph Blumhardt." In *The Beginnings of Dialectic Theology.* Vol. 1. Edited by James M. Robinson. Translated by Keith R. Crim. Richmond, VA: John Knox, 1968.

Barton, Michael, G. A. Clark, and Allison Cohen. "Art as Information: Explaining Upper Paleolithic Art in Western Europe." *World Archaeology* 26 (1994): 185–207.

Bass, Diana Butler. *Christianity after Religion: The End of Church and the Birth of a New Spiritual Awakening.* New York: HarperOne, 2013.

Bateson, Mary Catherine. *Composing a Life.* New York: Grove Press, 1989.

Bednarowski, Mary Farrell. "Lump in the Throat Stories." In *Arts, Theology, and the Church,* 50–70. Edited by Kimberly Vrudny and Wilson Yates. Cleveland: Pilgrim, 2005.

Berry, Wendell. *Recollected Essays: 1965–1980.* San Francisco: North Point, 1981.

boyd, danah. *It's Complicated: The Social Lives of Networked Teens.* New Haven, CT: Yale University Press, 2014.

Bregman, Lucy. *The Ecology of Spirituality: Meanings, Virtues, and Practices in a Post-Religious Age.* Waco, TX: Baylor University Press, 2013.

Chopp, Rebecca. *The Power to Speak: Feminism, Language, God.* New York: Crossroads, 1989.

Cleage, Pearl. *Deals with the Devil: And Other Reasons to Riot.* In *The New Georgia Encyclopedia Companion to Georgia Literature.* Edited by Hugh Ruppersburg. Athens: University of Georgia Press, 2007.

Cleveland, Christena. *Disunity in Christ: Uncovering the Hidden Forces That Keep Us Apart.* Downers Grove, IL: InterVarsity, 2013.

Coleman, Earle. *Creativity and Spirituality: Bonds between Art and Religion.* New York: State University of New York Press, 1998.

Cone, James H. *The Cross and the Lynching Tree.* Maryknoll, NY: Orbis Books, 2011.

———. *God of the Oppressed.* Rev. ed. Maryknoll, NY: Orbis Books, 1997.

Conkey, Margaret. "New Approaches in the Search for Meaning? A Review of Research in 'Paleolithic Art.'" *Journal of Field Archaeology* 14 (1987): 413–30.

Copeland, Adam J. "I'm #AmbivalentAboutFargo and You Should Be Too." *A Wee Blether* (blog). http://www.adamjcopeland.com/2014/06/09/im-ambivalentaboutfargo-you-should-be-too/.

———. "Is the PCUSA Going Down the Tubes?" *A Wee Blether* (blog). http://www.adamjcopeland.com/2013/09/05/is-the-pcusa-going-down-the-tubes/.

———. "Pastors Double Down on Facebook: The Boundary-Setting, Dual Identity of Pastors with Two Facebook Accounts." In *Media, Religion, History, Culture: Selected Essays from the 4th Elon University Media and Religion Conference*. Edited by Anthony Hatcher. Bloomington, IN: AuthorHouse, 2014.

Copeland, M. Shawn. *Enfleshing Freedom: Body, Race, and Being.* Minneapolis: Fortress Press, 2009.

Costen, Melva Wilson. *In Spirit and in Truth: The Music of African American Worship.* Louisville, KY: Westminster John Knox, 2004.

De La Torre, Miguel and Stacey M. Floyd-Thomas, eds. *Beyond the Pale: Reading Ethics from the Margins.* Louisville, KY: Westminster John Knox, 2011.

Derrida, Jacques. "The Ends of Man." In *Margins of Philosophy*. Translated by Alan Bass. Chicago: University of Chicago Press, 1982.

———. "Force of Law: The 'Mystical Foundation of Authority.'" In *Deconstruction and the Possibility of Justice*. Edited by David Gray Carlson, Drucilla Cornell, and Michel Rosenfeld. London: Rutledge, 1992.

———. *Of Grammatology*. Translated by Gayatri Chakravorty Spivak. Corrected ed. Baltimore: Johns Hopkins University Press, 1997.

———. "Semiology and Grammatology: An Interview with Julia Kristeva." In *Positions*. Translated by Alan Bass. Chicago: University of Chicago Press, 1982.

Dillard, Annie. *The Writing Life.* New York: Harper & Row, 1989.

Eckhart, Meister. "The Book of 'Benedictus': Of the Nobleman." In *Meister Eckhart: The Essential Sermons, Commentaries, Treatises, and Defense*. Translated by Edmund Colledge and Bernard McGinn. Mawhaw, NJ: Paulist, 1981.

———. "Counsels on Discernment." In *Meister Eckhart: The Essential Sermons, Commentaries, Treatises, and Defense*. Translated by Edmund Colledge and Bernard McGinn. Mawhaw, NJ: Paulist, 1981.

Foucault, Michel. *The Archeology of Knowledge and the Discourse on Language*. Translated by A. M. Sheridan Smith. New York: Pantheon Books, 1972.

———. *Ethics: Subjectivity and Truth*. New York: New Press, 1998.

———. *Michel Foucault: Beyond Structuralism and Hermeneutics*. Edited by Hubert L. Dreyfus and Paul Rabinow. 2nd ed. Chicago: University of Chicago Press, 1983.

García-Rivera, Alejandro. *A Wounded Innocence: Sketches for a Theology of Art*. Collegeville, MN: Liturgical Press, 2003.

Gutiérrez, Gustavo. *Spiritual Writings*. Edited by Daniel G. Groody. Maryknoll, NY: Orbis Books, 2011.

———. *A Theology of Liberation: History, Politics, and Salvation*. Edited and translated by Caridad Inda and John Eagleson. 15th anniv. ed. Maryknoll, NY: Orbis Books, 1988.

———. *We Drink from Our Own Wells: The Spiritual Journey of a People*. Translated by Matthew J. O'Connell. Maryknoll, NY: Orbis Books, 2003.

Halverson, John. "Paleolithic Art and Cognition." *The Journal of Psychology* 126 (1991): 221–36.

Huyssen, Andreas. *After the Great Divide: Modernism, Mass Culture, Postmodernism*. Bloomington: Indiana University Press, 1986.

Jenkins, Henry with Ravi Purushotma, Margaret Weigel, Katie Clinton, and Alice J. Robison. "Confronting the Challenges of Participatory Culture: Media Education for the 21st Century." MacArthur Foundation Reports on Digital and Media Learning. Cambridge, MA: MIT Press, 2009. https://mitpress.mit.edu/sites/default/files/titles/free_download/9780262513623_Confronting_the_Challenges.pdf.

Johnson, Luke Timothy. *The Writings of the New Testament: An Interpretation*. Rev. ed. Minneapolis: Fortress Press, 1999.

Jones, Tony. *The Sacred Way: Spiritual Practices for Everyday Life*. Grand Rapids: Zondervan, 2005.

Joseph, Chris. "State of the Art." Process, Trace Online Writing Centre. http://tracearchive.ntu.ac.uk/Process/index.cfm?article=131.

Keller, Catherine. *Face of the Deep: A Theology of Becoming.* London: Routledge, 2003.

King, Stephen. *On Writing: A Memoir of the Craft.* 10th anniv. ed. New York: Scribner, 2010.

Kingsolver, Barbara. *The Poisonwood Bible.* New York: HarperCollins, 1998.

Kleon, Austin. *Steal Like an Artist: 10 Things Nobody Told You about Creativity.* New York: Workman, 2012.

LaMothe, Kimerer. *Between Dancing and Writing: The Practice of Religious Studies.* New York: Fordham University Press, 2004.

Lamott, Anne. *Bird by Bird: Some Instructions on Writing and Life.* New York: Anchor, 1995.

———. *Traveling Mercies: Some Thoughts on Faith.* New York: Pantheon Books, 1999.

Lorde, Audre. "Portrait." In *The Black Unicorn.* New York: Norton, 1978.

———. "Poetry Is Not a Luxury." In *Sister Outsider: Essays and Speeches.* New York: Crossing, 2007.

McGiffert, Arthur Cushman. *Martin Luther: The Man and His Work.* New York: The Century Company, 1911.

Migliore, Daniel L. *Faith Seeking Understanding.* Grand Rapids: Eerdmans, 2004.

Mitchell, Beverly E. *Plantations and Death Camps: Religion, Ideology, and Human Dignity.* Minneapolis: Fortress Press, 2009.

Moschella, Mary Clark. *Ethnography as a Pastoral Practice: An Introduction.* Cleveland: Pilgrim, 2008.

National Writing Project. *Because Digital Writing Matters.* San Francisco: Jossey-Bass, 2010.

Norris, Kathleen. *Amazing Grace: A Vocabulary of Faith.* New York: Riverhead Books, 1998.

O'Connor, Flannery. "Letter to John Lynch, November 6, 1955." In *Flannery O'Connor: Spiritual Writings.* Edited by Robert Ellsberg. Maryknoll, NY: Orbis Books, 2003.

Powery, Luke A. *Dem Dry Bones: Preaching, Death, and Hope.* Minneapolis: Fortress Press, 2012.

Prensky, Marc. *From Digital Natives to Digital Wisdom: Hopeful Essays for 21st Century Learning.* Thousand Oaks, CA: Corwin, 2012.

Quintilian. *Quintilian on the Teaching of Speaking and Writing: Translations from Books One, Two, and Ten of the Institutio Oratoria.* Edited by James Jerome Murphy. Carbondale: Southern Illinois University Press, 1987.

Ricoeur, Paul. *From Text to Action: Essays in Hermeneutics 2.* Translated by Kathleen Blamey and John B. Thompson. Evanston, IL: Northwestern University Press, 1986.

Sharp, Melinda A. McGarrah. *Misunderstanding Stories: Toward a Postcolonial Pastoral Theology.* Eugene, OR: Pickwick, 2013.

Showalter, Elaine, Lea Baechler, and A. Walton Litz, eds. *Modern American Women Writers.* New York: Charles Scribner's Sons, 1991.

Shulevitz, Judith. "In God They Trust, Sort Of." *New York Times Sunday Book Review,* August 25, 2002.

Snider, Evan. "Teaching Document Design, Not Formatting Requirements." *ProfHacker* (blog). Chronicle of Higher Education. http://chronicle.com/blogs/profhacker/teaching-document-design-not-formatting-requirements/29041.

Sobrino, Jon. *A Spirituality of Liberation: Toward Political Holiness.* Translated by Robert R. Barr. Maryknoll, NY: Orbis Books, 1988.

Southall, Ashley. "A Twitter Message about AIDS, Followed by a Firing and an Apology." *New York Times,* December 20, 2013. http://thelede.blogs.nytimes.com/2013/12/20/a-twitter-message-about-aids-africa-and-race/?_php=true&_type=blogs&_r=0.

Stewart, Iris. *Sacred Woman Sacred Dance.* Rochester, NY: Inner Traditions, 2000.

Stone, Howard W., and James O. Duke. *How to Think Theologically.* Minneapolis: Augsburg Fortress, 2006.

Thistlethwaite, Susan. "Mary Magdalene to Rush Limbaugh: Your Apology Is Too Little, Too Late." *OnFaith.* http://www.faithstreet.com/onfaith/2012/03/05/mary-magdalene-to-rush-limbaugh-your-apology-is-too-little-too-late/10632.

Tracy, David. *The Analogical Imagination: Christian Theology and the Culture of Pluralism.* New York: Crossroad, 1981.

Vest, John. "#RoadtoEmmaus." Adventures in Post-Christendom, JohnVest.com. http://johnvest.com/2011/07/28/roadtoemmaus/.

Walker, Alice. *The Color Purple.* New York: Harcourt Brace Jovanovich, 1982.

Warrior, Robert Allen. "Canaanites, Cowboys, and Warriors." *Christianity and Crisis* 49 (1989–1990): 261–65.

Yaghijian, Lucretia B. *Writing Theology Well.* New York: Continuum, 2006.

Yarber, Angela. *Dance in Scripture: How Biblical Dancers Can Revolutionize Worship Today.* Eugene, OR: Wipf and Stock, 2013.

———. *Embodying the Feminine in the Dances of the World's Religions.* New York: Peter Lang, 2011.